DATE DUE

JUL 11 2007	
NOV 10 2009	
NOV 24 2010	
MAR 09 2015	

BRODART, CO. Cat. No. 23-221-003

America's Struggle for Same-Sex Marriage

America's Struggle for Same-Sex Marriage chronicles the evolution of the social movement for same-sex marriage in the United States and examines the political controversies surrounding gay people's quest for access to the civil institution of marriage. The book focuses on the momentous events that began in November 2003, when the Massachusetts Supreme Judicial Court declared unequivocally that the state's conferral of marriage only on opposite-sex couples violated constitutional principles of respect for individual autonomy and equality under law. The decision both triggered a political backlash of national proportion and prompted officials in San Francisco, Multnomah County (Oregon), Sandoval County (New Mexico), and New Paltz (New York) to issue marriage licenses to same-sex couples. The volume relies on in-depth interviews to provide an insider account of how courts, politicians, and activists maneuver and deal with a cutting-edge social policy issue, as well as real-life narratives about everyday people whom the debate immediately affects.

Daniel R. Pinello was educated at Williams College (B.A.), New York University (J.D.), and Yale University (Ph.D., political science). His scholarship includes *Gay Rights and American Law* (2003), *The Impact of Judicial-Selection Method on State-Supreme-Court Policy: Innovation, Reaction, and Atrophy* (1995), and "Linking Party to Judicial Ideology in American Courts: A Meta-Analysis,"*Justice System Journal* (1999). He is a professor of government at John Jay College of Criminal Justice of the City University of New York and has also taught at Ohio Wesleyan University, the University of New Orleans, and Yale University. Additional information on many of the court decisions discussed in this book may be found at www.danpinello.com, where the author maintains a free casebook on sexual orientation and the law.

AMERICA'S STRUGGLE FOR SAME-SEX MARRIAGE

Daniel R. Pinello
*John Jay College of Criminal Justice of
the City University of New York*

CAMBRIDGE UNIVERSITY PRESS
Cambridge, New York, Melbourne, Madrid, Cape Town, Singapore, São Paulo

Cambridge University Press
40 West 20th Street, New York, NY 10011-4211, USA

www.cambridge.org
Information on this title: www.cambridge.org/9780521848565

First published 2006

Printed in the United States of America

A catalog record for this publication is available from the British Library.

Library of Congress Cataloging in Publication data
Pinello, Daniel R.
America's struggle for same-sex marriage / Daniel R. Pinello.
p.cm.
Includes bibliographical references.
ISBN-13: 978-0-521-84856-5 (hardback)
ISBN-10: 0-521-84856-3 (hardback)
ISBN-13: 978-0-521-61303-3 (pbk.)
ISBN-10: 0-521-61303-5 (pbk.)
1. Same-sex marriage – United States.
2. Gay couples – Legal status, laws, etc. – United States. I. Title.
HQ1034.U5P55 2006
306.84'80973090511 – dc22   2005034448

ISBN-13 978-0-521-84856-5 hardback
ISBN-10: 0-521-84856-3 hardback

ISBN-13 978-0-521-61303-3 paperback
ISBN-10 0-521-61303-5 paperback

For Lee

Contents

Acknowledgments

This book would not have been possible without the unstinting generosity of the people who invited me into their homes and offices to conduct the eighty-five in-depth interviews on which the volume is based. They have my special gratitude.

Sundry public officials and interest group representatives generously gave me their time and attention. They were: in Massachusetts, state Senators Jarrett Barrios and Richard T. Moore, state Representatives David Paul Linsky, Liz Malia, Alice Hanlon Peisch, Kathleen M. Teahan, and Philip Travis, Somerville mayor Joseph A. Curtatone, Provincetown town clerk Douglas Johnstone, Mary L. Bonauto of Gay & Lesbian Advocates & Defenders, Tom Breuer and Ronald Crews of the Massachusetts Family Institute, Arline Isaacson of the Massachusetts Gay and Lesbian Political Caucus, and Marty Rouse of MassEquality; in San Francisco, Supervisors Michela Alioto-Pier, Bevan Dufty, and Aaron Peskin, Steve Kawa, Mayor Gavin Newsom's Chief of Staff, Chief Deputy City Attorney Therese M. Stewart, Deputy City Attorney Sherri Sokeland Kaiser, Kate Kendell of the National Center for Lesbian Rights, and Molly McKay of Equality California; in New Mexico, Sandoval County Clerk Victoria S. Dunlap and her attorney, Paul Livingston; in New York, New Paltz mayor Jason West and Evan Wolfson of Freedom to Marry; and in Oregon, Kelly Clark of the Oregon Defense of Marriage Coalition, Tim Nashif of the Oregon Family Council, Roey Thorpe of Basic Rights Oregon, and Tara Wilkins of the Community of Welcoming Congregations.

Equally essential to the volume were interviews with fifty same-sex couples who married in 2004. (As the introductory chapter explains, I'm at liberty to divulge only their first names.) In Massachusetts, Brent and Craig, Carol and Michele, Carrie and Danielle, Christine and Marianne, David and Doug, David and Yvan, Deborah and Michelle, Donna and Sabra, Gary and Richard, Heather and Katherine, Jack and Julian, Janine and Rebecca, Joseph and Keith, Joseph and Steven, and Linda and Sharon. In San Francisco, Anne and Simone, Bil and Kent, Craig and Geoff, Diana and Nancy, Gary and John, Gilbert and Richard, Jim and Ron, Jim and Simon, Joe and Marc, Judy and Kelly, and Lance and Sanders. In New Mexico, Barbara and Jaye, Claire and Harriet, Craig and Gregory, Ellen and Tracie, Gordon and Jeff, Peg and Spence, and PJ and Tony. In Oregon, Allen and Bill, Barbara and Deborah, Barbara and Heather, Brian and Douglas, David and Keith, Gabe and Michael, Gary and Rob, Herbert and John, James and Paul, Jennifer and Toni, Jim and Richard, Kalissa and Suzanne, Karleen and Kathy, Kathleen and Laurie, Laurie and Susan, Phillip and Raymond, and Sandra and Teresa.

Without external funding for the book's research, I bore the expense of travel and lodging to conduct interviews. Thus, indispensable help came from assorted good samaritans who provided free or low-cost housing during my trips around the country. In Massachusetts, Lori A. Johnson of Wellesley College acquainted me with George and Nancy Caplan, for whom I house-sat. Likewise, Joseph Stewart of the University of New Mexico found me the Albuquerque home of Christopher and Karin Butler during that couple's travel abroad. Professor Butler's parents, Beth and Chuck Butler, were wonderful hosts for my week in the Land of Enchantment. My fellow Williams College alumna, Sarah Taub, introduced me to Oregonian Brent Bolton, who made room available in his Portland home. Finally, Williams alum D. Christopher Kerby was a gracious host in San Francisco.

The single most important individual providing scholarly aid to the undertaking was Clyde Wilcox, who read the full manuscript. The book profited enormously from his generous and detailed critical commentary.

A precursor of chapter 3 was offered at the October 2004 "Legalizing Homosexuality" conference sponsored by the Sawyer Law and Politics Program of the Maxwell School of Citizenship and Public Affairs at Syracuse University. Keith J. Bybee and Thomas M. Keck were discussants and provided trenchant appraisals. A forerunner of the concluding chapter appeared as a paper at the 2005 Annual Meeting of the American Political Science Association, where discussants Mark A. Kessler and Sharon G. Whitney rendered invaluable critiques. Numerous other friends in academe also provided commentary essential to the project: Ellen Ann Andersen, Scott W. Barclay, Jay Barth, Michael J. Bosia, Susan Burgess, Sean Cahill, Michael Craw, Patrick Egan, Charles W. Gossett, Roger E. Hartley, Mae Kuykendall, Daniel Levin, Nathaniel Persily, Kimberly D. Richman, Ellen D. B. Riggle, Kenneth Sherrill, Glen Staszewski, Susan M. Sterett, Mark Strasser, Barry L. Tadlock, Zak Taylor, and Stephen Wasby.

Ed Parsons at Cambridge University Press shepherded the volume with consummate skill. A better editorial partner would be difficult to imagine. Stephanie Sakson, the production and copy editor, again provided the most sure-handed guidance transforming manuscript into book.

My colleagues at John Jay College of Criminal Justice of the City University of New York – George Andreopoulos, Janice Bockmeyer, James Bowen, Danette Brickman, James N. G. Cauthen, Rose Corrigan, Jack Jacobs, Barry Latzer, James P. Levine, Jill Norgren, Ruth O'Brien, Harold J. Sullivan, and Robert R. Sullivan – provided steadfast encouragement and support.

Lee Nissensohn, my domestic partner and – if the law ultimately permits us to marry – future husband, sustained this endeavor in every way. He has been my rock for eleven precious years.

Abbreviations

ACLU	American Civil Liberties Union
AG	Attorney General
API	Asian Pacific Islander
BRO	Basic Rights Oregon
COBRA	Comprehensive Omnibus Budget Reconciliation Act
ConCon	Constitutional Convention
DOMA	Defense of Marriage Act
FMA	Federal Marriage Amendment
GLAD	Gay & Lesbian Advocates & Defenders
HRC	Human Rights Campaign
Lambda	Lambda Legal Defense and Education Fund
LGBT	Lesbian, gay, bisexual, and transgendered
MCC	Massachusetts Catholic Conference
MFI	Massachusetts Family Institute
MGLPC	Massachusetts Gay and Lesbian Political Caucus
NCLR	National Center for Lesbian Rights
NGLTF	National Gay and Lesbian Task Force
OCA	Oregon Citizens Alliance
OFC	Oregon Family Council
SJC	Massachusetts Supreme Judicial Court

America's Struggle for Same-Sex Marriage

ONE

Introduction

VICTORIA DUNLAP WAS IN A DITHER. Someone called her office with a question she couldn't answer: Would she issue marriage licenses to same-sex couples?

In 2000, Dunlap was elected as the first Republican to the office of clerk of Sandoval County, New Mexico, in more than forty years. With the motto "Unity through Diversity," she campaigned as a reformer. The thirty-year incumbent clerk was leaving because of term limits and had handpicked her chief deputy to succeed her.

But Dunlap sensed a political opportunity, because the clerk's office was tinged with allegations of cronyism and corruption. Clerks run local elections in New Mexico, and the Sandoval County incumbent, employing questionable redistricting maneuvers, was accused of having thwarted people seeking public office. Moreover, her shop was under a consent decree regarding the supervision of Native American voting. Spending less than $1,000, while designing and painting her own campaign signs, Dunlap beat the chief deputy in a close election, with absentee ballots determining the outcome.

Dunlap and her husband have two children. An artist by trade, she sold her first painting at the age of seventeen and has a history of questioning the social and political order. As a high school student in Salt Lake City, she circulated a petition against the closing of local parks on the sabbath. The first real taste of politics came when she had to speak at a public forum on the Sandoval County schools. Her son had attention deficit disorder and was in a special education program with a particularly skillful teacher. But her house was redistricted away from that school, and Dunlap fought for her child to stay there under an open enrollment bill. She also had been a

Crime Watch activist and worked on EPA-regulated road-building projects.

Dunlap became a Republican because the party's local operatives were the most reliable in helping her to solve problems and because she admired New Mexico's progressive Republican governor, Gary Johnson, who promoted the decriminalization of drugs.

Once in office, Dunlap sought to modernize the operation. A big project was the digitizing of 1.8 million documents that the clerk maintains. She also mandated that her staff abide by the strict rule of law and find out the correct answers to questions that constituents asked.

So, in mid-February 2004, when a staff person received the question about same-sex marriage, it was forwarded to David Mathews, the county attorney, for an answer. Mathews's reply quoted state statutes ("Each couple desiring to marry in New Mexico shall obtain a license from the County Clerk and file the same for recording in the County issuing the license, following the marriage ceremony") and noted that the only gender-specific part of New Mexico marriage law was the application form created in 1961 (referring to the "male applicant" and the "female applicant"). The memo concluded with a suggestion to seek an opinion from the state attorney general.

Yet Dunlap's attempts to clarify New Mexico's marriage law were frustrated, as she explained:

> I pulled the law, which I do frequently. And I couldn't find [a prohibition of same-sex marriage] either. So I tried to make contacts with people that did know. I called the U.S. Attorney's office. I contacted Josh Akers at the *Albuquerque Journal* and asked him if he could get a hold of the governor. I called a contact in the state senate.
>
> The Secretary of State is generally one I can get answers from, because they're directly above me. They said that there was really nothing that they could do. People weren't responding to anything. This was almost like I had turned invisible. No one wanted to touch this.
>
> Josh Akers couldn't get a hold of the governor. I asked him to contact anybody he could, including the Attorney General,

whatever it takes. I can't ask for requests in writing from the Attorney General with this administration. I could with the prior administration. I think they changed policy or something. It has to be a legislator that makes requests. So you ask legislators.

And I'm frantically trying to find somebody that will figure this out for me. But nobody wants to go there with this one. And I'm a Republican. If I ask a Democrat senator, they're not even gonna. ... This state's so political. They'll just turn you off or maybe they'll set you up.

Dunlap sought an answer from other government officials for several days, but to no avail:

The U.S. Attorney's office was trying their best to help me out. They were the ones that were doing the most. But they said it wasn't within their jurisdiction. I thought maybe they could give me some leads.

But the time was coming where I knew that, if we had another call .... We really needed to figure this out. We were gonna have to do it. I was *not* gonna prevent someone from coming in here and getting a marriage license when they were obviously allowed to do so – at the point when I know that it's against the law to not allow someone a marriage license, ya know whatta mean? Then I must do it. I'm gonna always give them their rights.

So I had to make a decision, and I made a decision at that point. No one wanted to respond to it. I don't know what's going on here. I don't know why they're doing this. But I'm not gonna be responsible for denying anyone their rights. How was I to know that there weren't gonna be hundreds of people that were gonna be asking? I thought probably because of this thing that was going on in our country, they would be hitting all the county clerks.

I also had contact with the president of the association of clerks. He said the clerks had gotten together at one time or another, about ten years ago, and decided that they weren't gonna issue these licenses, based upon the application. I said, "An application does not the law make. We can't deny people rights based on an application." He said there was an Attorney General's opinion at one time. I said, "Where is that?" "I don't know. It's around here somewhere." I said, "That's a permanent record. You're not allowed to destroy an Attorney General's opinion. I need it by

3

Friday. Because by Friday, I will be issuing licenses." He said, "If I get it by Friday, will you stop?" "If it's the proper opinion, certainly. I just need clarification." Friday came around, and nothing. I didn't hear anything from anybody.

Dunlap decided to begin issuing marriage licenses to same-sex couples on February 20, and Joshua Akers broke the story to the media.

> I've always relied on the press, because they educate people. Evidently, Josh got with the AP to spread the word. And then we had all this thing happen.
>
> I told him, "I'm gonna separate the men from the boys here. I wanna know who's for this and who's against it. And I wanna know who's brave enough to stand up and say they are. Because I'm tired of politics."
>
> These are the people I serve. It's not the politicians. I need to know because I'm in the trenches here. We daily work with people. I could be the one needing the marriage license. Doesn't it mean anything to anybody? I have empathy for people. But no, it's all about politics. So I did it. And we had a great response.

Sandoval County has a population just under 100,000 people. Its clerk's office, in the backwater county seat of Bernalillo, some fifteen miles northwest of Albuquerque, usually issues no more than fifty marriage licenses per month. But February was different. On Friday, February 20, sixty-four same-sex couples obtained marriage licenses.

It was a one-day opportunity for New Mexico's lesbian and gay community. Too many people wanted to shut Dunlap down:

> I had so many people trying to manipulate me that day. I had all these people on the telephone constantly, calling from all over the country. I was astounded. And I'm really very low key. I just like to get my job done and get out.
>
> I had the Republican Party call me, and they were begging me to stop. I had the [county] commissioners begging me to stop. The chair sent me a memo and wanted to have this special meeting. They wanted to take responsibility for stopping me.

4

Both of them thought they knew it was against the law. Can you believe this? This is what I dealt with. Both of them thought that it wasn't lawful what I was doing. The unwritten law. You know, the honor-among-thieves kind of thing.

So they wanted to take responsibility for that. And since the Republicans wanna be like the Democrats, and the Democrats aren't about to let the Republicans win, I was being jerked around all day long, as to who was gonna make Victoria Dunlap stop. The Republican Party state chair called and asked me to stop. "If we get an opinion for you, and you do stop, will you say that we . . . ." It was like when these terrorists drop bombs and then they take responsibility. And I had to wheel and deal through that all day long.

Here were all these gay people that were so happy, and I was in a complete and total dither.

Craig and Greg

Greg* usually glances at the *Albuquerque Journal* online every morning. On February 20, Joshua Akers's headline, "Sandoval County to Allow Same-Sex Nuptials," surprised him. Greg, forty-nine, couldn't believe it was true. He telephoned the clerk's office to confirm the information, and then said to his partner, "Craig, the county clerk in Sandoval County is issuing marriage licenses to same-sex couples." Without a moment's hesitation, Craig, forty-seven, replied, "Let's go!"

Craig and Greg met on a New York City street. Their relationship, although delayed, seemed fated. Both moved to New York in 1980, but they didn't connect until ten years later. Craig was walking his Jack Russell terrier puppy and crossed paths with Greg, who was walking *his* Jack Russell terrier puppy. The two dogs were ecstatic to see each other and acted as if they were long-lost friends.

---

* The book's use of first names for gay and lesbian couples was neither their choice nor mine. Rather, the institutional review board of my employer, John Jay College of Criminal Justice of the City University of New York, administers the federal law that regulates how the college's researchers treat human subjects and mandated the first-name-only practice.

Indeed they were. They came from the same litter. Craig and Greg independently purchased the dogs from the same Connecticut breeder.

The two moved in together a year later, relocated to Los Angeles for a few years, and then returned to the New York area. Greg worked in advertising and taught school, but was most passionate about architecture and real estate. Craig is a librarian. Missing the West, the two looked for a less discovered city there and chose Albuquerque as a good opportunity: "When you leave the Northeast, you have some equity in your house, and you do well then in New Mexico, because the cost of living here is much less."

Craig and Greg made their first pass at marriage during the 1994 lesbian and gay March on Washington:

> There was a ceremony in front of the Treasury Building, a mass marriage on its steps. It had no legal weight. It was symbolic, to represent that this was one more thing that's being denied us.
>
> It was Greg and I and a thousand lesbians. I just remember being surrounded by women, without another male couple in sight.

Their second brush with marriage brought a sense of déjà vu. They drove the fifteen miles to Bernalillo early that Friday morning and found three lesbian couples in line at the Sandoval County Clerk's Office. Craig and Greg were the first male couple to apply for a marriage license in New Mexico.

Getting the license was just the beginning.

Greg: After we got the license, we had to get married. As soon as I got home, I called the Unitarian Church, because that's the only church I knew that might marry a same-sex couple.
Craig: We really knew that something was going to happen to stop this. We were not that naïve. So we wanted to have the ceremony and get the document back to be recorded as quickly as possible. This was Friday, and we wanted to be there Monday at nine o'clock to get the paperwork back. So there we were suddenly, with two days to find someone to perform a marriage.

Greg: That night, Basic Rights New Mexico [an organization formed in 2002 to fight a prospective ballot initiative seeking to overturn a 2001 state law prohibiting discrimination based on sexual orientation] jumped on it and set up a meeting at their office space for all the couples who got married. Someone called and told me about it, and we went there that night. When we got there, we found a minister who performed the ceremony. There were probably thirty couples there.

Craig: So we got married in this room basically full of total strangers. People were photographing it and videotaping it. It was so surreal and bizarre.

Greg: And it was very emotional. I think the emotion was probably just the shock that it was actually happening.

Craig: And so *fast!*

Greg: Even though I had gotten to the point where I felt that we should be able to get married, I figured it was going to be years away.

Craig: And if it had been legal earlier, I can tell you the way we got married wouldn't have been the way that I would have done it. I would have wanted at least one person I knew to be present.

Craig and Greg's marriage certificate was indeed recorded early the next week at the Sandoval County Clerk's Office, and it appears they are legally married under New Mexico law. They mused about what being married meant to them.

Craig: We've never wanted to have a church wedding and wear tuxedos. That's really not us at all. I've never had this lifelong dream to see myself in the church and all that. So I've never really felt that I was cheated out of any of that, because I never wanted it.

We've been together for thirteen years. Our bank accounts are all together. We've owned many properties in both our names. We've shared benefits. Our wills are written up. We have powers of attorney for each other for health purposes. So we've done all the papers and all the documents and all of that.

But that being said, you still don't really feel safe as a couple. Because you feel at some point, you may just be at the mercy of some person who's against us as gay people, that may not allow me to see him in the hospital or make a decision for him or whatever.

Greg: I had been putting a lot of thought into the whole marriage issue and talking to people. Some would say, "Civil unions, maybe. But I don't know. I just can't see same-sex marriage." Well, why? You know, the whole thing.

So then I started thinking to myself about domestic partnerships, civil unions, and all of that, and the ways that can give me a lot of the things I may be looking for. But also wondering how it plays into this whole psychology.

I have a cousin, a kind of activist lesbian in Connecticut. She was saying something about her father is okay with civil unions but not marriage, and she just knows it's because he's a goddamn bigot and is just antigay and all of this stuff. But that's his position. And that's kind of where I was going in my own thought process.

But you know what? Anything less than marriage really isn't enough. If civil union has all the benefits – every single one – that marriage gives you, it's still a different word. It's a different psychological thing. As gay people, we are not the same. We're different. We're less. Even if they try to make them the same, it's still the perception of having less. So the psychology of that was already brewing. And then when the Massachusetts court decision was rendered and that language was used ["The history of our nation has demonstrated that separate is seldom, if ever, equal"], I was like, "Yes! That's *it*!"

Craig: One thing that started miffing us off is that we only have one word for it: marriage. I think it would make it easier if we realized that we're talking about many things here. Marriage is a legal contract that two people can enter into. Now if they want to go and call that civil unions for *everybody*, that's what they should do.

Then if marriage refers to observing your religious beliefs, we have no problem with that. But when you say marriage, people don't realize it's all of these things tied together. It's the religious, it's the secular, the civil, the legal, all those things.

It suddenly hit us – it's really time for this to be straightened out. The United States is not supposed to be led by religious beliefs. If a church doesn't want to recognize a marriage between two men or between a white woman and a black man, that's fine within their religious beliefs. But from the governmental point of view, that distinction should not be made. It's between two adults who want to enter into this legal contract.

Greg: At one point, my brother even said to me, "Well, I don't think the Catholic Church should be required to marry gay people." And I said, "They don't have to! It's a *church*. They can marry whoever they want."

Craig: Catholics don't even believe in divorcing people. And that's a good analogy, flipping it over to divorce. A Catholic cannot get divorced within the Church. But that doesn't stop Catholics from getting a civil divorce and ending their marriage. According to their beliefs, if they still want to think they're spiritually tied, that's fine. But that has nothing to do in my mind with the legal aspect of terminating a marriage.

Peg and Spence

Peg and Spence have been together for twenty-three years. Peg, fifty-three, became a social worker in 1973. Spence introduced herself this way:

> I'm a good Catholic girl. I was born and raised here [in Santa Fe, New Mexico]. I come from a very old family here, of Hispanic descent. Our family is very well established. I'm the oldest of three children.
>
> My first career was as a social worker also. I dealt with children who had been abused and neglected. I did that in northern New Mexico, north of Santa Fe. Then I moved into social work administration. We opened the first adolescent treatment center in northern New Mexico for teenagers dealing with alcohol and drug abuse.
>
> And that's where I met Peg. I hired her. Convenient. I didn't have to go out and beat the bushes. We interviewed more than a hundred people. As I reviewed her application, I knew that we'd be together from that point on. Swear to God. Intuition.

Spence, fifty-four, is an attorney today and worked as a criminal prosecutor for twelve years before turning to civil practice, first with the state of New Mexico, now with the city of Santa Fe. She found out at work about Victoria Dunlap's decision to issue marriage licenses to same-sex couples:

Spence: Every morning, I routinely get on the Internet and check all three television stations to see if there's something in the news that might affect the city of Santa Fe. When I clicked on the CBS affiliate here [on February 20], I saw it. I called Peg and said, "You're not going to believe what's happening in Sandoval County. They're issuing marriage licenses to gay couples. What do you think?" We were like, "Ooohh. Let's go!"

We tried to think what to do when you plan a wedding, and stuff like that. Peg said, "When can you go?" I told her I was in court and couldn't get out until 1:30. So I met Peg at home at about 1:45.

We drove fast to Sandoval County. I didn't even know where the courthouse was. We looked for it and didn't see a whole lot of cars where we parked. I was afraid they'd already stopped. So we went into the courthouse and didn't see anything. We asked where you get marriage licenses, and they pointed upstairs.

Going up, we saw two gay guys coming down. They were carrying roses, and we asked them where to go. They said, "Upstairs," and gave us their roses, because we didn't have any flowers. We kept them. It was very sweet.

There was this long line of people upstairs. We were like, "Whoa!"
Peg: Very jubilant. Very high energy.
Spence: It was unbelievable what was going on. The excitement. The happiness.

There were probably a hundred people or so in line when we got there, anywhere from forty to fifty couples ahead of us. It was probably about 2:30 or 2:45.

It took forever. I felt so bad because everyone was so happy and excited, and I didn't want to put a damper on it by telling them, "You guys don't understand. You better move" [waving her hands in a "get along" gesture]. We were so afraid that somebody would walk in [and close it down]. It was awful. We were in line for about an hour.
Peg: There were a couple of ministers on the courthouse lawn doing marriages right off the bat. [Our minister] was the friend of two other lesbians we knew in line. They are Jewish and were going to be married by a rabbi. We knew that the [New Mexico] Attorney General was going to shut it down very quickly. So we were in a hurry.

The minister came over, and the four of us had a double ceremony, for time's sake. She married the four of us together. We sprinted back into the courthouse to get it registered before Patricia Madrid, the Attorney General, shut it down. And we made it by five minutes.

When we first got in line, people were getting the license part and then getting married. And everybody was just screaming and cheering.

But when we came out [of the courthouse for the last time], no one was hollering, because at least fifty couples had just been turned away.

Spence: And they had been jubilant. Just jubilant. And there were couples ahead of us who had their marriage licenses and were going off to plan huge weddings. They just figured that whenever they came back, they would record it.

Peg: Just like regular folk do. Straight folk go down, you get your license, you plan a wedding for June, you have a marriage, you sign it, and take it back or mail it to the courthouse, and they register it.

There was a couple in line behind us, who took our picture. We said to them, "Get married now. Get married right now. Get married *right now*." Then they decided to get married on the lawn, but were waiting for their teenage daughter and lolly-gaggling around. And they didn't get registered, because it was shut down.

Peg and Spence elaborated on the Sandoval County experience:

Peg: Being married, for me, is a spiritual piece, a commitment. The standing up in front of . . . . In fact, I was bemoaning that, of course, we couldn't grab our kids out of school. [In 1994, the couple adopted two siblings: a boy, three, and a girl, six.] We didn't have the time. I regretted that we had to rush and get married. Because what our marriage should have been about was inviting all of our friends and family to stand with us and honor this commitment that we have made for the past twenty-three years. So I made it into a spiritual event, especially with the minister doing it for us there, quickly, in less than five minutes, on the lawn.

I was kind of upset with Spence and the other two women we got married with. We went out to get a drink later. And all they were talking about was the political side of it. And I went, "People, take a breath. We just got married. We just got *married*. Look at *this* side of it." They blew me off completely. Still, it would be more important to me to be married in a church than it would be by a piece of dirt called the state of New Mexico. I'd still like to have something like that happen for the two of us.

I don't know if it's changed anything for us. If Spence had an accident in Oklahoma and was in an ICU, and if our marriage convinced some doctor or nurse that I should be next to her, then yeah, let me be a part of that. Of course, they'd have to call the sheriff anyway to keep me out. I wouldn't be leaving. They'd have to call security guards to pull me kicking and screaming out of an ICU, if she were laying there on the bed dying. That's what this is about.

There's also a poignant story from the time when Spence worked for the state of New Mexico. She had cancer then. I work for the state as well and hold a family health insurance policy. If Spence were a man, I wouldn't have even had to pay another dime. He would have been a part of the family policy.

Because of the circumstance of the cancer, Spence felt that she had to continue working, to keep the insurance for herself. All throughout her chemotherapy, she couldn't go on leave because we would've had to pay $300 a month for COBRA. So during chemotherapy, she was working full time.

I'm considering changing employment now, but I carry the insurance for our family. So that's a big consideration. How does Spence get insurance?

Spence: [A local reporter] interviewed me for an article and asked questions about what it felt like [in Sandoval County]. And I tried explaining what it was like to be at the courthouse. Then I said to him, "You can't even begin to imagine the types of emotions individuals were experiencing, because you [as a straight man] don't even have to have a second thought about being able to get married. To you, it's ordinary. To have something offered to gay people that they thought could never, ever be available, and all of a sudden, it was there. The emotions that were unleashed in Sandoval County were building up for centuries, from all the generations before us."

Gordon and Jeff

Gordon and Jeff live in a small town outside Santa Fe and are both college administrators. A lesbian couple driving to Sandoval County on February 20 telephoned Jeff, forty, to say that he and Gordon, fifty, should jump in their car and get married. The two men weren't able to leave until the afternoon and described what happened in Bernalillo.

Gordon: We had been there for about two hours, had wound our way through this long line, and were the third couple in line when the decision was made to shut it down.

The media were a little disappointed because they wanted some sort of TV moment. Instead, what they got was a very quiet, "OK, we knew this was going to happen. Sixty-some couples got through, and that's the plus. Now we're one step closer to where we want to be in this country. And that's a good thing." It was very orderly. There was one woman who yelled and screamed about its being unfair and wanted to excite the couples in line. But everybody was like, "This is the decision. We're a peaceful, gentle people."

Jeff: There was a lot of very visible disappointment. People were crying. All kinds of stuff. But there wasn't any riot.

Gordon: People just heard it, were hurt, stunned. They didn't leave for a long time because they kept hoping that some other outcome or interpretation would be forthcoming in a short time. And when it became clear that, no, it was really the end, people just went back to their cars.

Now the gay people who got married are the married couples. And people who were in line and disappointed are referred to [in New Mexico] as "the engaged." We are the third engaged.

Jeff: When we left for Sandoval County, our feeling was that we've been together nineteen years, we know what our commitment is to each other, and that this was just going to be something to go through to get this piece of paper. We really weren't emotionally connected with the idea of getting married. We hadn't thought about marriage. We never thought that we would see it in our lifetime. And so it hadn't really sunk in yet.

Then when we were in line, we just really formed this emotional attachment to the idea of marriage. Yes, this is something we deserve. And yes, we've worked hard for this. And why is our relationship less valid than that of a straight couple who have known each other for three days or three hours and can go to Las Vegas and get married?

Gordon: I was upset in January with the State of the Union address by President Bush and really angry at him. Then, when we added the emotional component . . . . Because it took the Sandoval County experience for me to say, "Now wait a minute. I am worthy. This *is* something important." There are all these other legal issues tied to marriage that domestic partnership doesn't solve, civil unions don't solve, all our legal paperwork doesn't even solve. Because we have wills, living wills, the whole nine yards. But it still doesn't handle lots of stuff.

Jeff: After the disappointment of being shut out [in Sandoval County], we talked about the issue on the drive home. The only other place at that point where gay people could get married was San Francisco. So we said, let's just do it. Marriage does mean something to us.

At home, we opened a bottle of champagne and toasted each other for getting as far as we did. Then we got online that night and booked a trip to San Francisco. We were planning on getting married on March 12, which was a Friday. We were flying in on March 11 and flying back out on Saturday. So it was just going to be two days.

The Monday after booking the flight, we found out that you had to have an appointment in San Francisco in order to get married.

Gordon: They were tired of the lines outside City Hall with thousands of people.

Jeff: I saw the new procedure on the San Francisco Web site, to call this number. We called for two days straight, sitting at work, just hitting redial, redial, redial. The line was busy for two days straight. We finally got through. I said, "I want to make an appointment for the twelfth." "That day is booked." "What is the latest you have on Thursday, the day before?" "The latest we have is a one o'clock." "We're flying into Oakland at ten o'clock. Can we get there in time? Because we're not familiar with the area." "Yeah, I think so. Oops! Somebody just booked the one o'clock. Well, I have noon now." "Book it! Just book it!" So he booked us at noon.

Gordon: Now we had less than two hours to get from the Oakland Airport to City Hall in San Francisco. That'll teach us to ask questions!

Jeff: A friend from college lives in Oakland, and I called her to ask if she could coordinate the trip to downtown San Francisco. And she was amazing. She had scouts in the airport to greet us. "Go this way! Go this way!" And she looped around the circle in front of the airport, pulled up, we jumped in, and she took off.

Gordon: She knew every shortcut between the Oakland airport and City Hall that there could possibly be.

Jeff: So she "got us to the church on time."

Gordon: She got us there so early that we had time to go to a taqueria for our wedding rehearsal dinner.

When we did the ceremony, it was an emotion-packed event. From the minute we walked in, I started filling up. Then, when they brought the flowers, that just sent me over the edge.

Jeff: People from all over the world were donating money for flowers for the same-sex newlyweds in San Francisco. So they had this huge basket that was full of beautiful flowers for us.

Gordon: It was assorted bouquets, and each was in a different color scheme. It was so amazing. The card just said, "To a loving couple." They were all anonymous. It was incredible to think of all these people who wanted to participate and be there in some way. So they were just sending money, and it was so thoughtful because we were an hour and a half off of a plane.

Then the ceremony was so profound and wonderful. We heard words that we've heard in movies and on TV a thousand times – "And now, by the power invested in me by the . . . ." – but to hear them said to *us* . . . . Tears were rolling down my face. I couldn't find my voice. Jeff started crying because he saw how upset I was.

Jeff: That got me going.

Gordon: The deputy commissioner of marriages, who does this all day long, started crying. We had to stop the ceremony so that he could find his voice again. It was just incredible.

One of the things we keep saying about all the gay marriages is that, unlike our straight friends who are having a celebration of what's in front of them, we have all the emotions and all the weight of our lives together. So we're celebrating what's in front of us, but we're bringing to that nineteen years behind us, too, that we're honoring and respecting, and acknowledging that commitment and time together.

Returning home to New Mexico, Gordon and Jeff wanted to share the news of their wedding celebration with friends and family.

Jeff: I sent a wedding announcement to my hometown newspaper, in a very rural county of Maryland. The publisher of the paper refused to print it, saying it wasn't legally recognized in Maryland. A young, emboldened editor decided instead, if they're not going to print the wedding announcement, they'll do a feature story on us. So he ran a page and a half story with seven photographs.

The couple also mused about the American political environment.

Jeff: It's frustrating that some people say that the right of gay people to marry needs to be put before the American people to vote on. It's only fair, they say, that the people get to voice their opinion. That kind of thing.

There were more people against interracial marriage decades ago than there are against gay marriage right now. But that didn't stop the Supreme Court from striking down laws banning interracial marriage [in *Loving v. Virginia* (1967)]. You don't make social progress by letting everybody vote on it.

Gordon: I was in Arizona when that state voted on the Martin Luther King holiday. And the country was outraged that people would vote against such an obviously worthwhile holiday.

What I always remind folks is: not only did Arizona vote against a Martin Luther King holiday, but it was the *only* state that had a popular vote on a Martin Luther King holiday. People in other states shouldn't be so cocky about how their citizens might have fallen on that question.

It wasn't until later, when Arizona lost the Super Bowl and there were other economic repercussions against the state, that they had to rethink and revisit that decision.

Aftermath

At the request of state senators, New Mexico Attorney General Patricia Madrid, a Democrat, issued an expedited advisory letter on February 20 that cited the 1961 application form and several New Mexico matrimonial statutes and court cases that refer to a "husband" and a "wife." Madrid concluded, "Thus, it appears that the present policy of New Mexico is to limit marriage to a man and a woman" and that "no county clerk should issue a marriage license to same-sex couples because those licenses would be invalid under current law."

On February 23, the Sandoval County Commission voted to allow all same-sex couples who received licenses on February 20 to register their marriages with the clerk's office.

At the request of the Sandoval County Commission and Attorney General Madrid, a state district judge signed a restraining order against Victoria Dunlap prohibiting her from issuing further marriage licenses to same-sex couples. That order remained in effect until the expiration of Dunlap's term as county clerk at the end of 2004, to which office she did not seek reelection.

The Sandoval County Republican Central Committee formally censured Dunlap, stating that she had "brought disgrace to the party as a whole." The committee's chairman noted before the vote, "Other than assassination, all we can do is censure her" (Akers 2004).

In March 2004, Paul Becht, a former Republican state senator, fundamentalist Christian, and New Mexico legal counsel for the Alliance Defense Fund, an evangelical Christian group, threatened to sue if the Sandoval County marriage licenses weren't nullified.

"The problem I have with same-sex marriage is it denigrates the whole idea of marriage. Living together and having sex together is not the definition of marriage," Becht said (McGivern 2004).

After her term as Sandoval County Clerk expired, Victoria Dunlap and her family moved to Ohio.

New Mexico as Introduction

How did same-sex marriage come to an obscure county of an out-of-the-way state? That turn of events depended in part on the presence of an unusual person as the clerk of the unsung county. But it also relied on the New Mexico lesbian and gay couples who prompted the clerk's action.

The Sandoval County experience with same-sex marriage serves as a primer for the country's battles over the policy in the first decade of the twenty-first century. A nongay public official made marriage licenses available to lesbian and gay couples, and they in turn flocked to take advantage of the opportunity. A political backlash ensued in other government branches, seeking to reestablish the prohibition of same-sex couples from the institution of marriage.

Parallels are suggested between gay people's fight for marriage rights and the African-American civil rights struggle and other social movements in American history. Religious and social conservatives deny that marriage for lesbian and gay couples is a legitimate civil rights claim and point toward a natural-law definition of marriage as between only one man and one woman.

This book explores these and other issues surrounding America's struggle for same-sex marriage. The research provides an insider account of how courts, politicians, and activists maneuver and deal with a cutting-edge social policy issue, as well as real-life narratives about everyday people whom the debate immediately affects.

TWO

Overview and Background

According to the U.S. Census Bureau, there were at least 600,000 gay and lesbian couples living together in the United States in 2000, in virtually every county in the country.

– Evan Wolfson (2004: 87)

NO ONE KNOWS FOR CERTAIN how many gay people are in the United States, because "[t]he gay and lesbian population is 'invisible'" (Riggle and Tadlock 1999: 6). During the 2000 elections, national exit polls indicated that 4 percent of voters self-identified as gay or lesbian. Yet that figure represents only those citizens who were prepared voluntarily to identify themselves as lesbian or gay to pollsters. Social scientists believe there's a large group of Americans who are at various stages of an ongoing process of "coming out" as gay or lesbian. In any event, the 600,000 same-sex households reported by Wolfson above indicate that the population is substantial.

This book chronicles the evolution of the social movement for same-sex marriage in the United States and examines the political controversies surrounding it, particularly during the momentous time that began on November 18, 2003.

That day, the Massachusetts Supreme Judicial Court (SJC) decided the landmark case of *Goodridge v. Department of Public Health* and declared that the Commonwealth's conferral of civil marriage only on opposite-sex couples violated the Massachusetts constitution's principles of respect for individual autonomy and equality under law. Less than three months later, on February 3, the

SJC, in *Opinions of the Justices to the Senate,* ruled that civil unions, even with all of the state-conferred rights and responsibilities of marriage (but not the name), were an inadequate remedy for the constitutional breach found in *Goodridge.* Massachusetts's high tribunal thus became the first American court of last resort to hold unequivocally that lesbian and gay couples have a constitutionally protected right to marry.

Nine days after *Opinions,* on February 12, San Francisco mayor Gavin Newsom instructed the San Francisco county clerk to issue marriage licenses to same-sex couples. By March 11, when the California Supreme Court ordered San Francisco to cease and desist, 4,037 pairs had received licenses. San Francisco's "month of marriages" put the first public face on married lesbian and gay couples, garnering enormous national media coverage of the City Hall events.

In turn, San Francisco triggered a countrywide cascade of similar actions on same-sex marriage by local officials that flooded airwaves and bandwidths. As elaborated in the introductory chapter, Victoria Dunlap, the clerk of Sandoval County, New Mexico, issued sixty-four marriage licenses to gay and lesbian partners on February 20. Mayor Jason West of New Paltz, New York, officiated at the weddings of twenty-four same-sex couples on February 27. On March 3, four of five Multnomah County commissioners authorized the issuance of marriage licenses to same-sex couples in the Portland area of Oregon, and in the next seven weeks, more than 3,000 lesbian and gay pairs received them there. Finally, on March 8, City Clerk Dawn Tomek issued marriage licenses to seven same-sex couples in Asbury Park, New Jersey. Thus, in February, March, and April, more than 7,000 marriages among same-sex partners occurred in the United States.

A month later, on May 17, pursuant to the *Goodridge* decision, Massachusetts began issuing marriage licenses to lesbians and gay men there. In the course of the next year, an estimated 6,000 or more same-sex couples were wed in the Bay State.

These events triggered a nationwide wave of reaction. On January 20, 2004, in the State of the Union address to Congress, President George W. Bush condemned "activist judges" who were "redefining marriage by court order." Then, on February 24, after same-sex weddings began in San Francisco and Sandoval County, President Bush endorsed a congressional proposal for this amendment to the federal Constitution:

> Marriage in the United States shall consist only of the union of a man and a woman. Neither this Constitution or the constitution of any State, nor state or federal law, shall be construed to require that marital status or the legal incidents thereof be conferred upon unmarried couples or groups.

The Federal Marriage Amendment failed by substantial margins in both houses of Congress in 2004. The Senate vote to invoke cloture, or end debate on the measure, was 48 to 50 – far short of the two-thirds' majority (67) needed for federal constitutional amendments. Among the 435 seats in the House of Representatives, at least 290 must approve of changes to the national charter. But the FMA tally was just 227 to 186.

Yet state constitutional amendments banning same-sex marriage passed with broad voter approval in thirteen states that year. Moreover, state supreme courts invalidated the gay and lesbian marriages in California and Oregon, holding that Mayor Newsom and the Multnomah County commissioners exceeded their authority in directing the issuance of those licenses. Last, the Massachusetts Legislature took the first of three steps to amend the state constitution to limit marriage to one man and one woman but at the same time to authorize civil unions for same-sex couples with all of the state-conferred rights and responsibilities of marriage.

That's the story in a nutshell. Subsequent chapters on Massachusetts, California, Oregon, and New York greatly enlarge this outline. The Appendix explains my empirical methods.

Hats

Writing this book, I wear several hats. The first and most prominent is that of narrator. As the introductory chapter illustrates, participants in same-sex-marriage events around the country in 2003–2004 tell their tales here. My job is to collect and to present those stories in the unvarnished words of the people who lived them.

At the same time, I'm a professor of government who studies law and courts from a political science perspective. So my second function is that of scholar analyzing these collected narratives in America's struggle for same-sex marriage.

Last, I'm a gay man in an eleven-year relationship with another man. Hence, my perspective on same-sex marriage isn't disinterested. But I've made every effort not to allow my personal interest in the subject matter inappropriately to influence the discharge of these other responsibilities, which, by far, are dominant in the volume.

This last hat served both as an advantage and a disability in researching the book. Given my long-term interest in gay-rights issues and prior scholarship on how American courts treat gay litigants (Pinello 2003), I had unique entry to the lesbian and gay interest groups that helped to spur the movement for same-sex marriage. Virtually everyone in those organizations whom I asked to interview, including central figures behind gay Americans' quest for marriage, in fact met with me.

By the same token, my being gay was essential to achieve access to the fifty same-sex couples across the country whom I interviewed for the book (see the Appendix for particulars about them). Many responded to my initial interview requests by asking whether I myself were gay and saying they wouldn't be willing to see me if I weren't. Thus, I don't believe a nongay researcher could attain an equally successful response from the couples.

At the same time, my status as a gay professor who researches gay rights and the law probably diminished the willingness of interest group leaders opposing same-sex marriage to meet with me. I didn't achieve nearly the same level of access to them as I did with the gay groups. I recount a related experience as evidence of the problem. I invited thirty members of the Massachusetts Legislature to be interviewed. Included in the request was my curriculum vitae, which not only reveals my scholarship on gay rights but also my membership in the Lesbian, Gay, Bisexual and Transgender (LGBT) Caucus of the American Political Science Association. So anyone reading the document carefully would have a good idea of who I am. Half of the legislators I asked to interview voted in favor of a state constitutional amendment banning same-sex marriage in the Commonwealth, while the other half opposed it. Five (or 33 percent) of the fifteen in the latter group agreed to be interviewed, while only two (13 percent) in the former did so. In short, politicians favoring same-sex marriage were about two and a half times more likely to meet with me than those who oppose it. The same was true of interest groups fighting same-sex marriage.

Early Stirrings

The first gay male couple to apply for a marriage license, in May 1970, was Jack Baker and J. Michael McConnell. The clerk of Hennepin County, Minnesota, denied their application, and the next year, the Minnesota Supreme Court held that the men had no federal due process or equal protection rights to marry (*Baker v. Nelson* 1971). The first marriage case involving a lesbian couple arose in Kentucky and met a similarly unsuccessful fate (*Jones v. Hallahan* 1973).

At least four more failed attempts to seek judicial recognition of same-sex marriage occurred in the next two decades (*Singer v. Hara* 1974; *Adams v. Howerton* 1980; *De Santo v. Barnsley* 1984; and *Dean v. District of Columbia* 1992). As one commentator observed, "legal agitation for gay marriage in the 1970s [and '80s] was a complete flop" (Eskridge 1999: 135). Another noted:

> [C]ourts narrowed the issue to that of "gay marriage" as opposed to the claim of marriage as a fundamental right advanced by the [same-sex] plaintiffs. By defining the issue as same-sex marriage, courts were able to "simply" look at the definition of marriage, determine that marriage means a relationship between a man and a woman, and reject the claim as incompatible with the definition. (Dupuis 2002: 43)

It's no wonder these early lawsuits miscarried. Lone couples, unsupported by organized lesbian and gay interests, made ad hoc assertions of novel social and constitutional positions, often without the benefit of legal arguments orchestrated by seasoned advocates.

Nonetheless, the circumstances behind the cases, as well as their outcomes, would soon change.

The Mastermind

If anyone can be credited as the principal architect of gay people's struggle for legal access to the civil institution of marriage in the United States, it's attorney Evan Wolfson. As a student at Harvard Law School in 1983, Wolfson wrote the first extensive legal analysis of the issue, in a paper titled "Same-Sex Marriage and Morality: The Human Rights Vision of the Constitution" (Garrow 2004).

Despite his own prescient usage of the term "same-sex marriage," Wolfson began our interview with a request about this book's title.

You really have to stop calling it "same-sex marriage." It's not about same-sex marriage. It's about marriage. Calling your book something like *The Struggle for Marriage and Same-Sex Couples* would be more accurate.

We, as gay people, are seeking marriage, but the fight in the country isn't really over marriage rights for gay people. In truth, the struggle is about gay people. The opponents here are antigay, not just anti–marriage equality. What's transforming the country is coming to terms with, and accepting, gay people and their love on terms of equality.

Marriage is the vocabulary and the terrain and the important legal structure at the center of this struggle. But by no means is it the only issue. And it's not just a matter of words. "Same-sex marriage" suggests that we're trying to change something or invent something new or other or lesser. And that's just not true.

In the California case [challenging the state's limitation of marriage to opposite-sex couples], [San Francisco Superior Court] Judge Kramer made a great statement at the opening of arguments [in December 2004], to the effect that, "The dispute in this case is less about what marriage is than who gets to have the benefits of getting married." That's what this is about – who gets entrance into marriage. Same-sex couples, not same-sex marriage. Okay?

So try *Marriage and Same-Sex Couples*. Same thing. Everybody will know what the book's about.

After graduating from law school, Wolfson started volunteering for Lambda Legal Defense and Education Fund, the nation's leading lesbian and gay legal advocacy organization. Then, he joined Lambda as a full-time staff attorney in 1989.

One of the rare areas in which there was disagreement among the very small band of legal activists doing gay rights work around the country then was the question of whether to pursue marriage. That's something we began debating and fighting over pretty early on in my tenure. The division didn't exist just among Lambda's attorneys, but within the larger Lambda family – advisers, advisory committees, the board, and so on.

Lambda also worked with colleagues in other small organizations, such as GLAD [Gay & Lesbian Advocates & Defenders] in Massachusetts, the National Gay Rights Advocates in California, now defunct, and a very small group called the Lesbian Rights Project, which became the National Center for Lesbian Rights. These groups communicated and worked together. We met regularly, which actually started a few years before I came on staff. So even as a pro bono attorney, I was attending meetings of what has become known as the Roundtable.

Again, marriage was one of the very few things over which people really fought. The divisions were of two kinds. One was ideological, those who really believed that we should be talking about this and fighting for it, because marriage was important and a powerful vocabulary. Those people thought that one couldn't support equality without being in favor of marriage.

A larger group within the activist corps at that point either wasn't that interested in marriage or was outright dismissive or disdainful of it, believing instead that we should be fighting for other kinds of family recognition. The phrase used was "redefining the family."

Then, in addition to the ideological divide, there was a different division cutting across those strategic lines. These people, who may not have shared the dislike of marriage or the resistance to the marriage work, felt that it was too much too soon, or too hard, or that it would trigger a backlash, or in order to get there, you had to take various small steps.

So there were these two divisions, and that wasn't just within Lambda. That was across the activist community. Marriage was the subject of many heated arguments. Our position evolved through a lot of wrangling and fighting at several of the round-tables when this was on the agenda. They were some of the more contentious and difficult meetings.

What really, of course, changed things was Hawaii.

In May 1993, the Hawaii Supreme Court rendered a landmark decision in *Baehr v. Lewin*. The plurality opinion held that the limitation of marriage to opposite-sex couples constituted discrimination on the basis of sex, in violation of the Hawaii Constitution. Hawaii's high tribunal thus became the first court of last resort in the country to adopt a constitutional principle as a legal basis for the marriage of same-sex couples.

Wolfson sketched the history behind the *Baehr* ruling and its aftermath.

In the early 1990s, potential plaintiffs in Hawaii contacted me to ask if I would handle their case. Mutual friends told them about the paper I wrote as a student and that I was an advocate for marriage equality. The gay movement, to that point, had been relatively unsuccessful at getting legal groups and others to take the marriage issue up. So they contacted me to ask if I would represent them.

Three couples, with some local activists, wanted to bring a lawsuit. They believed there was potential for success in Hawaii. Of course, I wanted to do it. But when I brought the case to my colleagues at Lambda – we decided things collectively – it was rejected. I was told I couldn't do it.

That turned out to be one of the luckiest days the movement has ever had, as I wrote in my book, because it brought the couples to Dan Foley ["a well-known and respected civil rights attorney in a small Honolulu firm" who "previously served as legal director of Hawaii's ACLU affiliate." Foley "was one of the state's top constitutional lawyers" (Wolfson 2004: 30–31).].

Meanwhile, back at Lambda, we continued to argue about marriage, as the Hawaii litigation began and moved forward. I was speaking about the case, calling attention to it. Once the lower court ruled against us, and Dan [Foley] and his couples appealed to the Hawaii Supreme Court, I was able to persuade my Lambda colleagues that, at that point, it was appropriate.

I should explain first that, although I wasn't authorized to take the Hawaii case, I was permitted to brainstorm and provide advice, as we would for any gay case. Thus I had been in contact with them, trying to help shape the litigation, although not terribly so because there wasn't that much then. Once the case went to the Hawaii Supreme Court, I was able to persuade my colleagues to do a friend-of-the-court brief. We also did an *amicus* brief in the D.C. case [*Dean*] that began around the same time. Those were Lambda's first briefs in marriage cases, and they laid the groundwork for further discussion.

Once the Hawaii Supreme Court ruled, I came back with much greater force to my colleagues at Lambda and then to the circle of the Roundtable and then beyond that. I got support each time, from the legal groups to the political organizations, with this Paul Revere message: "Whatever you thought before, the world has just changed. This is a major ruling. A court has said that, unless the government can show a good reason why same-sex couples shouldn't be married, the state constitution requires it. Now is our time to make that case forcefully. Also, this is not just about a court decision. This is going to be a titanic struggle and opportunity, culturally and politically, in tandem with the legal side."

From that point on, I was out there, now with the support of Lambda, and soon with the backing of other legal groups, who understood the implications much quicker than some of the political groups and other activists.

Wolfson mused about the lessons of Hawaii.

My colleagues in the legal groups who were resistant [to litigating marriage] were not necessarily wrong, even about Hawaii. We got lucky in the Aloha State. In fact, had the litigation made it to the state supreme court as it was composed at the time Dan and others started the lawsuit, we would have lost. There happened to be changes in the composition of the court, really just within a few months of the case making it there, that brought us a baby-boomer bench that was ready to hear it. That was just a matter of luck. So one lesson is, sometimes you get lucky.

Thus, on the one hand, those in the gay legal "establishment," which was a very small and beleaguered group to begin with, had to appreciate the occasional value of a maverick [such as Dan Foley and the Hawaii activists] and the importance of chance. But you also have to work to make room for luck.

On the other hand, the people in Hawaii, the lawyer-activist team, did very little to prepare for what was coming. They fortunately found a brilliant and wonderful attorney to file their case. But if Dan had turned it down, they would have gone to another attorney who wouldn't have brought to the litigation what Dan did. Yet even with Dan's incredibly wonderful assets – which weren't just as a lawyer, but knowing the political scene in Hawaii and helping to steer through shoals that lay ahead – they did nothing to equip Dan and the team to follow through.

As a result, Hawaii mounted this tremendous political resistance and counterattack and challenge that, on the ground there, we were completely unprepared to meet.

In the spring of 1997, the Hawaii Legislature proposed a state constitutional amendment ("The legislature shall have the power to reserve marriage to opposite-sex couples") for the ballot, and 69 percent of Hawaii voters ratified it in November 1998. As a result, the Hawaii Supreme Court dismissed the *Baehr* litigation the next year. Yet in the wake of *Baehr*, the state legislature in 1997 created a "reciprocal benefits" law that granted limited relationship rights to same-sex couples.

Wolfson described how Hawaii's lessons impacted the gay rights movement.

First the legal groups, and then the political and movement organizations, and then the state groups in collaboration with national organizations, were brought together around a one-sentence statement of support for a position and a focus on, and regular meetings around, something – a proactive, sustained campaign approach to issues. That had never happened before.

That was a big change in how movement organizations did business and communicated with each other. For example, there had been no gathering of the then relatively small state organizations to get them into one loop, together with the nationals, to talk about how matters could play out state-by-state and what they could be doing affirmatively and not just reactively. There literally had never been such a culture.

So we laid the foundations for what has now become the Equality Federation of statewide groups, the coalition that began meeting regularly – and by regularly, I mean about every six weeks over a period of years. That had never happened before. So that was a major change in the movement.

Another was the effort to go out in the public and frame something, to take a lawsuit and say, "Here's what's coming. Now you need to do this in this community. You can do that in that community. We'd like to give you tools to do this here, so that you can talk to nongay people to prepare them for a case that's coming from somewhere else." That had never happened before either.

It was an attempt not to see things as one case or one battle or one issue. Rather, it was all about the cause, and the way to use a vocabulary, and the engagement to talk wherever we are in order to move public opinion in support of what's coming legally, trying to get ahead of the legal. That was new to the movement.

The next consequential legal action in the struggle for same-sex marriage occurred in 1999, when the Vermont Supreme Court, in *Baker v. State*, ruled that limiting marriage to opposite-sex couples violated the state constitution's "Common Benefits Clause," or equal protection provision.

Wolfson welcomed the six-year hiatus between the Hawaii and Vermont decisions.

I think it was a good thing. We timed that pretty much right. We were very conscious of, on the one hand, the desirability of having enough legal work to drive the discussion forward and to prompt the organizing, while on the other hand, not having the litigation get too far ahead of the public education and political coordination. We were very attentive to that question, and I think that was fine.

When we ultimately decided to proceed with another case, in Vermont, we did so in part because we felt then that the additional value in moving the legal work would be greater than any potential increase in the attacks and ferment that the case might trigger.

In other words, there was some advantage in having Hawaii be where it was – big and exciting enough to stimulate activity on our side to get things going, as well as coming on the radar screens of our opponents, who already had been attacking us in waves for decades, and this was now another surge. But Hawaii wasn't so threatening and imminent that it would tip that balance in the wrong way.

Whereas we couldn't have filed, say, twenty more cases. We just wouldn't have been ready for them in terms of public education and political organization. We were getting enough bang out of the Hawaii decision to provoke more public discussion without needing other legal vehicles. Moreover, when filing lawsuits, you're turning the decision over to courts, and if a court rules against you, then you're done there.

Eventually, in 1995 and 1996, our opponents fiercely attacked us in Congress and announced this formal campaign to go state by state. The national debate rose to the kind of level it's at again now [in 2004]. Interestingly, people today have conveniently forgotten how intense the controversy was in 1996.

Indeed, that year, Congress passed, and President Bill Clinton signed, the Defense of Marriage Act (DOMA), which defines marriage as a "legal union between one man and one woman as husband and wife," limits federal benefits (e.g., Social Security survivor benefits) to opposite-sex couples, and seeks to enable states to refuse to recognize same-sex marriages performed in other jurisdictions. At that time in the mid-1990s, states also began adopting their own local DOMAs. By 2005, forty had legislation or state constitutional amendments banning same-sex marriage.

In 2000, in the wake of *Baker*, the Vermont Legislature passed a civil unions law, granting more than three hundred relationship rights and obligations to same-sex couples. The Vermont Supreme Court agreed that the new statute was an adequate remedy for the violation of the common-benefits provision of the state constitution. Civil unions thus became the first comprehensive legislative attempt, albeit prodded by court action, to approximate marriage for lesbian and gay couples, while avoiding the label of marriage.

Political Science Themes

I think historians will view the developments in the social and political evolution toward same-sex marriage documented in this book to be as momentous as the 1969 Stonewall Rebellion that touched off mass protests by newly self-identified, out-of-the-closet lesbians and gay men (Marotta 1981; Duberman 1993) and that sparked the modern gay rights movement. Moreover, as a political scientist, I believe these events in substantial measure are a micro-cosm of the American legal and political universe. Accordingly, I use the same-sex marriage narratives here as a prism to study three recurring themes in political science.

The first is the role and impact of courts in a democratic society. An enduring research topic in democratic politics is the nature and functions of governmental institutions. The impact of Congress and of the presidency on the polity, for instance, is a standard theme among scholars studying American politics. Few observers dispute that legislatures and executives generally are powerful and con-sequential foundations of the state.

The scholarly literature in political science, however, reveals a conspicuous absence of consensus over whether American courts are important governing institutions with their own distinct power. On the one hand, Dahl (1957), in a seminal article, argued that, despite popular belief about the United States Supreme Court's checking other branches of government, the Court in fact is an integral part of the political regime and often assists in imposing majority will on minorities. But, Dahl noted, "[b]y itself, the Court is almost pow-erless to affect the course of national policy." Scheingold (1974) warned that reformers' reliance on rights and litigation was grounded on a mythical and unrealistic idea of what they could accomplish. Rosenberg (1991) investigated what rights litigation in the Supreme Court achieved as an empirical matter and concluded that the Court is structurally incapable of producing significant social reform, with the implication that courts generally are inconsequential as actively governing institutions.

On the other hand, McCann (1994) and various authors in Schultz (1998), as rejoinders to Rosenberg, offered alternative perspectives and methodologies for inquiry about how courts can effect social reform. The resultant legal mobilization model argues that social movements can use law as a means to mobilize supporters, generate publicity, and educate the public to achieve social change.

The centrality of the *Goodridge* decisions to the same-sex marriage events of 2003–2004 is apparent from even this chapter's brief overview and will be fleshed out in later ones. The SJC's rulings invite analysis of their impact in light of the scholarly debate on judicial efficacy.

The second political science theme in the volume is the participation and impact of interest groups in a pluralist polity. Gay & Lesbian Advocates & Defenders (GLAD), in Boston, and Lambda Legal, headquartered in New York City, were the lesbian and gay public interest law firms serving as lead counsel and *amicus curiae* in the same-sex marriage lawsuits in Hawaii, Vermont, Massachusetts, and elsewhere. Other national organizations (e.g., the Human Rights Campaign (HRC), the National Center for Lesbian Rights, and the National Gay and Lesbian Task Force (NGLTF)), as well as sundry state and local groups (e.g., Basic Rights Oregon and Marriage Equality California), substantially augmented the fervor for same-sex marriage.

At the same time, organized opposition to gay marriage developed in kind, with national groups such as the Family Research Council, Focus on the Family, and Liberty Council spearheading that effort and strengthened by state affiliates such as the Massachusetts Family Institute and the Oregon Family Council.

In short, the marriage debate provides a marvelous prism to observe interest group strategy and policy warfare. On the one hand, GLAD and Lambda prompted courts to acknowledge constitutionally based marriage rights for same-sex couples, while HRC and NGLTF fought legislative retrenchment in the form of DOMAs and the Federal Marriage Amendment. On the other hand, organizations such as the Alliance for Marriage and the American Center for Law and Justice resisted altering the legal and political status quo on marriage, and where changes such as domestic partnerships and civil unions occurred, sought reinstatement of the status quo ante.

The last theme considers the sources of, and political responsiveness to, policy initiative in American government. As mentioned, the Hawaii Supreme Court's 1993 *Baehr* ruling sparked a feeding frenzy of hostile local and national reaction, resulting in the passage of DOMAs by Congress and more than thirty state legislatures in the 1990s. Then Massachusetts's *Goodridge* decisions spurred a flurry of supportive activity among nongay political entrepreneurs, such as Mayors Newsom and West and diverse city commissioners and town clerks. In turn, those events provoked President Bush's endorsement of the Federal Marriage Amendment, which announcement then led to even greater protest by lesbian and gay activists.

This two-step around same-sex marriage supplies compelling commentary about how domestic policy originates and evolves in the United States.

THREE

Massachusetts

The courts are our grammarians in the large sense of nourishers of the genius of democratic speech. They challenge the coarseness of the public vacuum about gay lives by forcing to the surface the idiom in which gay lives are lived.

– Mae Kuykendall (2001: 1031)

WHAT HAPPENS POLITICALLY once courts enter the fray surrounding hot-button social issues such as same-sex marriage? Before 2003, the answer with regard to that topic was: Only political disaster befalls interest groups and other supporters who prevail in court – a modified version of the *Hollow Hope* argument (Rosenberg 1991) at the state level.

Witness the Aloha State after the 1993 Hawaii Supreme Court's *Baehr* ruling. Political backlash crushed the nascent same-sex marriage moment there, with only very modest reciprocal benefits ultimately accruing to gay and lesbian couples. More important, Congress passed the Defense of Marriage Act in 1996, and more than three dozen state DOMAs ensued.

Then came the Vermont Supreme Court's 1999 *Baker* decision and the Vermont Legislature's endorsement of civil unions the next year. Later in 2000, Republicans resoundingly took control of the Vermont House of Representatives, where sixteen incumbents who supported civil unions lost reelection (Moats 2004: 260).

This chapter tells the story's third installment.

Massachusetts before *Goodridge*

The struggle for same-sex marriage in Massachusetts has roots that go back at least to 1989, when the Commonwealth became the second state in the nation (after Wisconsin in 1982) to include sexual orientation in statewide laws banning discrimination in employment and public accommodations.

The Massachusetts Gay and Lesbian Political Caucus (MGLPC) has lobbied on behalf of the Commonwealth's LGBT community for three decades and was instrumental in facilitating the 1989 statute. The group next moved to improve the legal rights of lesbian and gay couples. Arline Isaacson, MGLPC's longtime co-chair, described these efforts.

Domestic partnership was a piece of legislation that the Caucus filed with the legislature back in the early 1990s. When we acted then, we didn't expect the bill to pass for many years. We were filing it as a consciousness-raiser and thought that legislators eventually would get around to understanding it.

When we filed domestic partnerships, we had divisions within the LGBT community over how we would frame and spin it. Back then, we argued, if you sell this as a relationship issue, it will go down the tubes faster than you can bat an eye. If you sell it as equal work for equal pay, then you can give legislators permission, if you will, to be uncomfortable with gay people, or even be homophobic. But they would have to be more than homophobic to oppose this framing. They would have to be anti-union or anti-labor. They would have to be anti-fairness. And that is a much higher hurdle.

So we would say to legislators who we knew would not be at all comfortable with gay folks, "Look, whatever you think of us, it doesn't really matter. Think of two secretaries doing the same work. One is a straight woman who was just hired on the job and married last year with a brand-new husband. And the other secretary is a twenty-year employee who's a lesbian in a twenty-year relationship. And you're going to treat the one-year employee more favorably than the twenty-year employee?"

And they could get it. Everyone could get it. They might not like it, they might not agree, but they could get it. And most would end up saying, "Yeah, that's kind of hard to justify, isn't it? That is egregiously wrong." The reason I say this now is that the more we focused on benefits, the more palatable this question was to people who aren't comfortable with gay folks. And the more we focused on equality and, in particular, equal benefits, the easier it was for people to swallow. Because you have to be a real SOB to not want someone to be equal, even if you really don't feel that way. But most people can't admit that to themselves, far less to somebody else. And most people don't want to believe they are a bigot or prejudiced. Legislators are no different from anyone else in this regard.

So that was domestic partnerships in the '90s. We knew we had to consciousness-raise for a while and that the legislature would never pass it. Even if it did happen, all it would do would be to grant us domestic partnership health insurance. And that's it. Yet it was viewed then as highly radical. But nonetheless, it was a vehicle that allowed us to start talking about the injustices, inequalities, and inequities that gay folks suffer from in the work environment, and in a fashion that was hard for opponents to resist.

After the Vermont struggle precipitated by *Baker*, interest groups opposing same-sex marriage suspected that it was only a matter of time before the issue arose through litigation in other states. The Massachusetts Family Institute (MFI), for example, had been a sponsor since 1998 of a statutory DOMA in the Commonwealth. GLAD commenced the *Goodridge* lawsuit in April of 2001. In response, opponents sought to amend the state constitution to ban same-sex marriage.

Massachusetts's charter may be revised two ways. First, an amendment may originate within the General Court (the legislature's formal name). The proposed change must receive simple majority votes from among the 200 state legislators meeting in constitutional convention in two successive legislative sessions. Then the measure goes to the next general election. Thus, if a legislatively initiated constitutional amendment got at least 101 votes in, say, both the 2004 and 2005 "ConCons," it would be placed on the November 2006 ballot.

The other way to amend the Massachusetts charter is by citizen initiative. Proponents of a measure must secure a designated number (57,100 as of 2001) of voter signatures on petitions. Once the signatures are certified by the Commonwealth, at least 25 percent of (i.e., 50) state legislators meeting in constitutional convention in two successive sessions must also approve the initiative. Then the referendum appears on the next general election ballot.

Moreover, in the charter-amendment process, the Massachusetts Constitution gives the senate president absolute authority as to when constitutional conventions are convened and as to what their agendas are.

In the fall of 2001, same-sex marriage opponents began to gather signatures on petitions outside supermarkets, Target stores, and churches throughout the state. Over 130,000 signatures were collected, and about 79,000 were certified by the Commonwealth – 20,000 more than needed to transfer the initiative to the next ConCon.

Yet, as the first order of business at the summer 2002 ConCon, then Senate President Thomas Birmingham recognized a colleague whom he had prepositioned to make a motion to adjourn immediately, even though representatives and senators supporting the antigay ballot measure raised their hands and shouted to be recognized to call for a vote on the citizen initiative. The motion to adjourn passed, but with 53 recorded "no" votes. Thus, had the convention considered the merits of the marriage referendum, enough of the 200 lawmakers would have voted in favor of it in order to continue the process of sending the measure to the people. However, the ConCon's failure to act on the initiative killed it.

Hence, the 2002 ConCon lasted just a few minutes. Nevertheless, several hundred supporters of the ballot proposal sitting in the statehouse spectators' gallery erupted into shouts of "Let the people vote!" – so much so that security guards became alarmed and made everyone leave the gallery. All the same, a mob of protestors moved to Senator Birmingham's office door and continued to shout, "Let the people vote!"

The two sides explained this ostensibly enigmatic legislative frustration of the popular will differently. Ronald Crews, MFI president, said that his sources warned that Birmingham wasn't going to allow the vote to happen and that the senate president refused before the ConCon even to meet personally with initiative proponents. Crews noted that Birmingham was then running for governor and wanted to prove his liberal bona fides for Democratic voters in the upcoming primary. Furthermore, citizen initiatives for constitutional amendments are rarely successful in Massachusetts history. As an institutional matter, the General Court seeks to preserve its policy-making authority.

Supporters of same-sex marriage offered a far different account for the abrupt adjournment of the 2002 ConCon. MGLPC put together the strategy to stop the antigay constitutional amendment in the 2001–2002 legislative session. LGBT activists thought that they could never win a popular vote then and that their only chance was to convince the legislature not to take the issue up. Arline Isaacson described the frame of mind at the time.

> When we were first faced with the constitutional amendment to ban same-sex marriage back in the 2001–2002 legislative session, it was unequivocally clear that there was no chance of winning at the polls whatsoever. The only question was, by how much would we be slaughtered? Not that we would lose by a little, because that wasn't an issue. Rather, it was that we were going to get massacred, and by how much would we be annihilated.
>
> Therefore, our strategy then was radically different from the approach we use now [2004]. In 2001 and 2002, when confronted with the first ballot question for an antigay constitutional amendment, not a law, our strategy was, "Don't talk about the M-word." Because the M-word was the third rail. It was the issue that would burn legislators and advocates alike. It was simply not supported by more than a very tiny percent of the legislature.

The first element of the MGLPC strategy to combat the citizen initiative was to document systematic fraud that went into collecting the 130,000 signatures on ballot petitions. The Caucus formed "truth squads" that monitored the signature gathering. (Truth-squadding is sometimes known as "decline-to-sign" campaigns.)

Again, Arline Isaacson:

The referendum's financial backers had picked a signature gathering company that was hired to collect signatures on this and several other petitions. One of the others had to do with the prevention of the slaughter of horses. So nice, kind, animal-loving people would see pictures of Black Beauty displayed around a card table in a shopping center and would be lured over to the table by these paid signature gatherers with shouts of "Save the Horses! Sign our petition!" And people would come over and say, "Oh yes, save the horses. I'll be happy to sign." Then the signature gatherer would say, "What town are you from?" "I'm from Quincy." "Oh here, let me get you the Quincy page," and he'd turn to the "Quincy page" and say, "Sign right here." And guess what. The animal lover wasn't signing the horse petition anymore, but was signing the antigay one.

In addition to this bait-and-switch trick, they did the sign-twice ploy. "You know the government. It's so bureaucratic. You have to sign two copies of our petition, because one has to go to D.C. and the other to Beacon Hill." There was this panoply of different tricks they used.

When the signatures were certified, we took all the names and put them up on a Web site and said to people, "Go to the Web site. See if your name is there." And we started getting calls from people around the state who said they never signed a petition against same-sex marriage.

In fact, the signature-gathering company failed to collect enough signatures for the Save Our Horses campaign, which sued in state court claiming fraudulent conversion of signatures from its petition to the marriage one (Ebbert 2002). Although MGLPC's truth-squadding wasn't adequate to knock the marriage initiative off the ballot through administrative and judicial means, its effort did eat away at the credibility of the referendum organizers, as Isaacson concluded: "These people were not passionate volunteers, caring only about democracy in action, but rather were paid signature gatherers who committed fraud on a regular basis. So that made some legislators more open to doing what ended up happening in 2002."

The second element in persuading the General Court to reject the ballot measure focused on its breadth. Not only did the initiative define marriage as just between one man and one woman, but it also denied any kind of benefits (such as health insurance for domestic partners) to same-sex couples. That broad language provided the opportunity to characterize the referendum as overreaching and mean-spirited. Arline Isaacson:

> Our opponents could have gone just for marriage. But they were greedy, God bless them, and they went for marriage and benefits. That was the best gift they could have given us. So then we were able to lobby legislators for benefits, and whatever you think about marriage, it doesn't matter. This was about benefits, and you have to be a real SOB to say that gay people can't have health-care benefits. So a key component in winning during the 2002 Constitutional Convention was "benefits, benefits, benefits." That was our mantra. And we studiously avoided the M-word, which was a vote loser then. So we won the ConCon, and legislators were able to talk about benefits during the 2002 election campaign.

When the fate of the 2001–2002 citizen initiative was becoming clear, MFI and the Massachusetts Catholic Conference (MCC) prepared a legislatively initiated amendment banning same-sex marriage as their backup plan. They asked Democratic Representative Philip Travis, from a conservative district in southeastern Massachusetts, to be the lead sponsor, and he agreed. Hence, the opponents of same-sex marriage seized on a legislative approach for the 2003–2004 election cycle, rather than go through the expense and time of getting signatures again.

Despite the 2002 experience, same-sex marriage wasn't high on the radar screens of most Bay State politicians before the fall of 2003. Alice Hanlon Peisch, a Democratic house member representing the affluent suburban towns of Weston and Wellesley, offered a typical assessment.

> The question [of same-sex marriage] came up very peripherally in my [2002] campaign. I was aware of what Vermont had done with respect to civil unions. To the extent that I gave the matter

any thought, my view was that people should be treated equally. I thought that the civil union concept made sense. I recall someone asking me about marriage, and my response was that I thought that was so unlikely to be presented to the legislature that I really hadn't given it much thought. I was more interested in supporting something that I thought had some viability. So I didn't want to waste my time on something that I thought was pretty unlikely to receive much in the way of support. And then I didn't frankly give the matter another thought. It was not something that was a key issue in my campaign.

Moreover, the house leadership and the Judiciary Committee were dominated by social conservatives. Speaker Thomas Finneran was a traditional Irish Catholic politician who reflected the policy preferences of his church and conservative district. And the Massachusetts speaker casts a long shadow over the statehouse in Boston. The more populous house chamber has 160 members, while the state senate consists of only forty.

Indeed, prior to *Goodridge*, the legislature would have been lucky to pass domestic partnership benefits statewide, let alone something more comprehensive such as civil unions. Representative Liz Malia, one of two openly lesbian and gay lawmakers at the statehouse in 2003, summed up the experience of progressive legislators then.

Our discussions were mostly around domestic partnership benefits. And that had been the battle for the last few terms. The most we had really focused on – not that we didn't have aspirations to do civil unions or whatever – but we were finding it very difficult even to have, and thought we'd be very lucky to get to the point of having, an open debate on the floor to discuss domestic partnerships realistically.

I think it's probably pretty fair to say that, with some intensive discussions with leadership, where we thought we would be able to move would be toward domestic partners, but with DOMA language. Those were the signals I thought we were getting from the leadership [in 2003]. In my mind, we were basically looking at civil unions. We were starting to have those discussions, but it was always with a caveat, as far as the opposition was concerned, with regard to the definition of marriage. That was the key step that always got in the way of coming to final agreement.

I think that we had really hit a stalemate before the *Goodridge* decision arrived. We knew that the potential was out there and basically had decided that we couldn't compromise with a DOMA, with the definition of marriage. And that seemed to be as far as the leadership was willing to go. I think we were in neutral at that point in time.

Goodridge

Both sides in the debate over same-sex marriage fully participated in the *Goodridge* litigation from the beginning. GLAD's Mary Bonauto selected the seven plaintiff couples from across the Commonwealth to represent the class of gay men and lesbians seeking state-sanctioned civil marriage. The suit began in the Massachusetts Superior Court in April 2001.

The Massachusetts Family Institute was also there, as its President Ronald Crews explained.

We filed as *amicus curiae* at the Superior Court level and also at the SJC [Supreme Judicial Court]. In both of those, we helped to coordinate all of the *amicus* briefs that were going to be filed, in terms of planning sessions about what points we wanted to raise and what organizations would be the most readily available to address those points, in assigning different attorneys different tacts to take. At the Superior Court level, we had about eight or nine briefs. At the SJC level, I think we eventually filed fifteen or sixteen briefs.

I was a part of the planning process of what it would be that we wanted to say, and who was the best person to write a particular point, of assigning the points out around the country, to various law schools and professors and persons who have been engaged in this battle in other venues, like Vermont and California.

We worked closely with organizations like the Alliance Defense Fund, the Liberty Council, the American Center for Law and Justice, and other national organizations that we knew wanted to have *amicus* briefs. We had several meetings here in the Boston area where they sent representatives, and we would talk through the briefs.

The plaintiffs' strategy for presenting legal arguments to the courts was equally orchestrated. In fact, GLAD may have been more successful at recruiting the state's legal establishment to its cause. Most of the Commonwealth's legal elite, for example, supported the plaintiffs, with *amicus* briefs filed on behalf of the state's two major bar associations, the Boston Bar Association and Massachusetts Bar Association. Moreover, the attorneys writing other *amicus* briefs (representing distinguished local and national experts on federal and state constitutional law, on the history of American law and the family, on child welfare, and on other relevant topics) indicate that GLAD did substantial outreach to the largest and most prestigious law firms in the Commonwealth. These documents may have provided the justices an enormous comfort zone, because people at the top of their fields (both social scientific and legal), and mostly based in Massachusetts, were collectively saying to the court, "Yes, marriage."

The SJC took an unusually long time to decide the case. Oral argument occurred on March 4, 2003, and the court's 4-to-3 decision was rendered more than eight months later, on November 18. In the interim, the U.S. Supreme Court, in *Lawrence v. Texas*, announced that the liberty provisions of the federal Constitution protected the private sexual intimacies of adult same-sex couples and overruled *Bowers v. Hardwick* (1986).

Reaction to *Goodridge* was predictably mixed. MFI's Ronald Crews was surprised and outraged:

> Gerry D'Avolio, the Executive Director of the Massachusetts Catholic Conference, and I had a meeting with Senate President [Robert] Travaglini in early November [2003]. In that meeting, President Travaglini said he fully expected the court to "kick the ball" to the legislature. He was fully anticipating that they would not make the decision they did.
>
> We knew that it would be a divided court. Going in, based on the way the justices asked questions during the oral argument, we thought, leaving there, that there were two, Chief Justice

[Margaret] Marshall and Justice [John] Greaney, who were solidly going to vote to create so-called homosexual marriage. We were pretty sure of two who were going to say "no." So that left three, and we didn't know how they would come out. So we were confident it was going to be a split decision, but we just didn't know how it was going to turn out.

The court was audacious to make such a radical decision. They just totally ignored the rational basis for marriage. They pretty much said there's no rational basis for defining marriage with a heterosexual component, just ignoring law, precedent, history, social science, biology. For me, the audacity and the radical nature of the decision were just stunning.

Further, I was one of the people who had been vocal that Chief Justice Marshall should recuse herself because of the comments that she had made at a fundraiser for GLAD prior to this decision's working its way up to her court. Here she speaks at a fundraiser saying the Vermont Supreme Court did not go far enough. That says to me that a judge is prejudicial to a case coming before her. I'm still stunned that she has been able to get away with that. I've seen the tape of the speech that she made, and it was recorded in the *Boston Globe*. And she didn't even get one of the other justices to write the majority opinion. She did it. That to me was stunning and a surprise.

The majority also totally ignored and dismissed the arguments of the dissenting justices. Several law professors I've spoken with have indicated that the minority opinion was written as though it were the majority. It's longer than the majority. It is more well reasoned. It's based more on legal precedent and history. Some speculation is that they wrote it thinking they were the majority opinion, and something must have happened just at the last minute, with one of the justices changing the vote. But who knows. The reality is we got what we got.

Representative Travis, the principal legislative opponent of same-sex marriage in the Commonwealth, was so offended by the SJC's handling of the *Goodridge* case that he sponsored a bill to remove Chief Justice Marshall from the court.

When we tried to offer civil unions as suitable in Massachusetts like Vermont, not only did [the Chief Justice] say [in *Opinions of the Justices to the Senate]* that it didn't go far enough, she commented sarcastically in the tone of "When is the legislature going to smarten up? When are the senators going to come around to the fact that this is a fait accompli?" Read her decision and read between the lines. "Don't dare give me something like this. I don't want to deal with superfluous things when I'm going for marriage." It's very offensive to read her decision.

The Senate wanted to find a middle ground early on so we could do it legislatively. She just closed that option to us by saying, "No. I interpret the constitution as saying marriage is anything."

Even voices that were ultimately sympathetic to the *Goodridge* outcome expressed astonishment. David Paul Linsky, a Democratic member of the Massachusetts House of Representatives from a moderate district in Natick and Sherborn, is an example.

A: The way I read the court, they decided it solely on the Massachusetts Constitution, and there's no mention in the entire decision of the federal Constitution. The Massachusetts Constitution has a clause called the Free and Equal Clause, where all people are created free and equal. The court has consistently interpreted that clause to go beyond the federal Constitution's Bill of Rights and its equal protection clause to give people more freedom and more rights in Massachusetts than under the federal Constitution. Yet I still think it was a reach for anyone to think that they would use that to overturn something as basic as marriage. We were just shocked and surprised that they did it. I'm glad that they did. But I think it was an amazing reach.
Q: Is there anything about the composition of the court that would help to explain the outcome?
A: The Chief Justice grew up in South Africa. She was clearly influenced by apartheid there. You've got an African-American on the court, Justice [Roderick] Ireland, who voted in favor of same-sex marriage. The majority of the court is appointed by Republican governors. There is a libertarian streak in all of them, and they take civil liberties very seriously. That's what it's about.

Goodridge also disconcerted Alice Hanlon Peisch, the legislator who hadn't given much thought to same-sex marriage after it came up only peripherally in her 2002 campaign:

> I didn't think about [same-sex marriage] again until the *Goodridge*
> decision came down. And I was surprised at that. I expected that the
> court would act similarly to the Vermont court and require that
> there be some equity with respect to rights and benefits, but that civil
> unions would be acceptable. When the decision was initially handed
> down, we all wondered about what this 180 days meant. [The court
> stayed the enforcement of its decision for 180 days "to permit the
> Legislature to take such action as it may deem appropriate in light"
> of the decision.]
>
> Many of us, myself included, hoped that we could fashion some
> piece of legislation that would confer equal rights and benefits but
> not use the word "marriage," because the backlash on marriage,
> at least from my perspective, was very strong. I thought that, at
> the end of the day, it would be less helpful to advocate for
> that position even if it went through. I was encouraged that the
> Senate president followed the procedure that the Massachusetts
> Constitution allows for the legislature to inquire of the court as to
> whether certain bills would pass constitutional muster. Just before
> we were to enter into the Constitutional Convention, the SJC
> ruled that, no, civil unions were not good enough.

The 2004 Constitutional Convention

The *Goodridge* decision significantly altered the playing field for
advocates on both sides of the same-sex marriage controversy.
Before November 18, 2003, the burden of responsibility politically
to change the status quo rested with LGBT activists, that is, to
persuade the General Court to pass domestic partnership benefits or
civil unions or whatever. However, once the SJC announced that the
state constitution mandated same-sex marriage, the onus settled on
opponents to restore the status quo ante. Representative Linsky
summarized the shifting burden and demonstrated its very
consequential effect.

> All of a sudden, the *Goodridge* decision came down from the SJC,
> and I think everyone was, quite frankly, surprised the way that

45

they came down. And then the issue became, all right, the SJC says that same-sex marriage is legal. It's required under the constitution. And no legislation is necessary. And then it would take a constitutional amendment to take away the right of same-sex marriage.

So then this issue was framed very much differently from the legislative standpoint. For me, it came down to, well, could I possibly vote for a constitutional amendment that takes away a right of some people who live in Massachusetts? And that is something I, quite frankly, could just never do – take away a right. Because I honestly think that the constitution, be it the Massachusetts Constitution or the federal Constitution, is a place for the listing of rights rather than a restriction on rights. And then I saw this as a civil right. And there was just no way I could ever vote to take away a civil right.

So that was my legal analysis. That was the part of me that was a lawyer looking at this and saying, "This is what I have to do legally. I can't vote to take away any rights. I'll have to oppose the constitutional amendment."

Accordingly, *Goodridge* significantly transformed the procedural posture of the debate, empowering those who effectively had been politically powerless before.

Yet although a court decision had prompted the procedural necessity for the February–March 2004 ConCon, same-sex marriage advocates in the legislature felt prepared to defend the *Goodridge* outcome on the merits before their colleagues. Representative Malia made the point the following way.

People here [in the General Court] who were probably neutral or skeptical about anything understood that we had made serious attempts on numerous [past] occasions. There was a real legislative history, trying to bring this issue to debate and to the floor. We were stalemated, and it wasn't going to happen with existing leadership on any level that people would be satisfied with.

For those of us who aren't attorneys, a real basic concept of government is that, if you're not able to make any progress through the legislature, which is the first venue you have access to, then eventually somebody's going to go to the courts, and rightly so.

Representative Peisch, who is an attorney, agreed.

> I think the court was doing what it's supposed to do. Now from a
> political standpoint, it would have been easier for all of us if they
> had done something differently. But at the end of the day, they're
> appointed to interpret the constitution, that's their job, and they
> did it. And people who criticize them for being "activists" and
> usurping the role of the legislature .... Well, the legislature had
> plenty of opportunity to act on this question. For many years,
> there have been bills filed to deal with this. Probably because the
> leadership was not supportive of this issue, those bills never got
> out of committee. So it's a little bit disingenuous of some people
> around here to be complaining that somehow a court stepped in
> and took away our authority.
>
> If you look at the federal Constitution and the Supreme Court,
> this is a role that the courts have played for a number of years. I
> don't think it's inappropriate. I know there are those who do.
> Schools wouldn't be desegregated, we wouldn't have a lot of the
> civil rights that we take for granted today if the courts had not
> interpreted the Constitution to enforce the rights that are guar-
> anteed in it.

LGBT activists had learned important strategic lessons from the
2002 ConCon. Some felt, for instance, that they had been politically
outmaneuvered when same-sex marriage opponents outnumbered
supporters at the statehouse during legislative deliberations.
The "Let the people vote!" choruses from the house spectators'
gallery and in front of Senate president Birmingham's office
were still fresh in activists' minds. Marty Rouse recalled that
moral and his response as campaign director for MassEquality, the
umbrella organization directing response to political backlash from
Goodridge.

> I was told that several years ago when this happened the last time,
> our opposition was in the halls all the time. They were putting
> pressure on the legislators, chanting and singing. It was a strong
> presence for them. Our supporters felt overwhelmed that the
> opposition had outnumbered us in the statehouse. There wasn't a

strategy for us to be in the statehouse then. So that was one of the things people told me when I came on board here. We needed to be sure to have a presence in the statehouse during the next constitutional convention.

So we sent e-mails out, here's when the doors open, here's what you should do, be prepared to do this, be prepared not to do that, here's how you should engage yourself and how you should talk to people and not talk to people. We informed supporters how to come to the statehouse and be prepared to do X, Y, and Z. In the event that people didn't know the words to "God Bless America," we handed out song sheets. We had lots of flags. We had lots of water. Lots of breath mints, lots of cough drops to soothe the throat.

We came prepared to be in the statehouse for twelve hours each day. And supporters appreciated how much we cared about them, gave them water, told them when to take breaks, gave them soda and chips. What we did was very coordinated and strategic. We sang patriotic songs and chanted.

And it was really memorable – the volunteers who were there, both inside the statehouse and outside the chamber, all day, singing. From seven or eight o'clock in the morning, until midnight, almost nonstop, "God Bless America," "America the Beautiful," "This Land Is Your Land," and some civil rights songs, all day long. Those memories, along with waving American flags, and having signs saying "No discrimination in the constitution," standing outside the chamber, being a voice, a physical presence, letting the legislators know, "We are the face. You can vote however you want to. But we are the people you are impacting right now." And being that face and maintaining a vigil outside the chamber while they voted, even knowing we probably were going to lose – that was really empowering to see how the supporters who were there understood their role. I think they were transformed and felt powerful.

Of course, the most important audience for this political theater was the legislators themselves. The demonstrations and outreach by the LGBT community before and during the Constitutional Convention directly affected David Paul Linsky.

I got to see, for the first time in my life, more and more and more examples of gay and lesbian couples, who had been together a long time, and people for whom this was a very personal issue and had a real effect on their lives. In addition to that, I got to know more and more same-sex couples who live in my community, because they were starting to reach out to me to talk about this issue, including one of my wife's best friends, who is involved in a committed lesbian relationship. And from a previous marriage, she has two sons, one of whom is one of my son's best friends. This was starting to really hit home, quite frankly. Because that kid is at my house all the time, and my son is over at their house all the time. I was realizing that this is really a significant issue for a whole lot of people that I care about very deeply.

In addition to that, the statehouse, during the time that led up to the Constitutional Convention, and during the convention itself, was flooded with people on all sides of this particular issue. I was realizing how many people this truly affected in a deeply personal way. And I can't do anything to ever hurt anybody, and I want to do things to help people. So I made a decision that I was going to be out there on this issue, and I was going to fight as hard as I possibly could. And I'm extremely glad that I did, because it was the right thing to do.

For me, it culminated in a couple of points during the Constitutional Convention. One was that – and this happened throughout the convention when hundreds and hundreds and hundreds of people demonstrated in front in favor of same-sex marriage – they were gathered on a balcony in the statehouse, and throughout the Constitutional Convention, they were singing patriotic songs. It was so moving. At one point during a break in the convention, I went out there with several of my colleagues, just to listen and to talk to people, and it was incredibly, incredibly moving.

And then when it came time for me to speak to the Constitutional Convention, my original plan was to restate the legal analysis that I had prepared weeks before. At the last minute, I decided, no, I'm not going to do that. Instead, I talked about two things. I talked about the people who were singing and the effect that had on me. And I talked about some of the people in my town that I knew who were deeply and personally affected by this issue. And I talked about my son's friend.

Yet LGBT activists relied on more than just singing and demonstrating at the statehouse. They also incorporated more traditional lobbying techniques, as Marty Rouse, one of MassEquality's staff of two at the time, detailed.

The most important thing that MassEquality brought to the table was the organization of a movement outside the statehouse. So legislators weren't just being targeted inside the statehouse. We made sure that we mobilized constituents. The Catholic Church, on the opposition, was very well organized, because they have people coming to mass every Sunday. What we needed to do was mobilize just like that. And it wasn't easy. Being a grass-roots and political organizer, my job was to find ways to mobilize people outside the statehouse. Where do we go? Which districts are most important? Who's with us? Who's against us? Where are the movable people, and how do we organize within those districts?

We used e-mail very effectively. We used the Internet tre-mendously to get people motivated to contact their legislators. "Want to know who your legislator is? Just type in your address here and find out. Here's her phone number, call in, and say this. Spread the word to five friends, let us know whom you're con-tacting." We spread this far and wide.

Sure enough, what happened during the Constitutional Con-vention was, when we first got started in January, the phone calls were ten to one, or twenty to one, against us. With every day that went by, slowly but surely, more supporters were calling. And that's because we were finding more people and urging them to call their legislators. And that's what we were doing, building a movement outside the statehouse to contact key legislators stra-tegically. So by the time we got to the Constitutional Convention, legislators were feeling the heat on our side as well, and were feeling that they had our support and that there were people out there supportive of what they were doing. They knew then that they had some power to vote against the amendment.

And while we thought we would lose three to one or two to one at that first vote – we counted only about thirty votes, out of two hundred, on our side – we ended up getting actually about fifty or sixty. And by the time the final vote came, we had eighty-four friends. We actually built a movement of support. That's what MassEquality did. We became an identified force, inside *and* outside the statehouse. That's never ever been seen before [in the LGBT community] in the Commonwealth of Massachusetts.

Representative Liz Malia elaborated on the LGBT lobbying strategy and how activists sought to expand the profile of gay people whom marriage potentially affected. The first constituency was children.

There are families here. It doesn't matter whether you approve of it or not. There's kids here, and they have a future.

A [former legislator] who got to be a good friend [is] a judge now in the Boston area. He was an old-fashioned Democrat, but pro-life and conservative on a lot of social issues. But [also] very thoughtful. I remember him saying [to me], "Once you guys got adoption, then it was all over." Because he's a major kids-rights and pro-family person. And he took that literally, in terms of being pro-family, and saying, "Now we're talking about the welfare of kids." And that pushed him to start thinking about, "How do we deal with this? Whether I like it or not, this is where we are at in society. These issues will come up. It's time to move past my own personal values."

And I saw people like him moving. A lot of folks I think really started to see, "This isn't a bunch of wild-eyed, crazy people out in the street protesting. This is my next-door neighbor."

Another segment of the LGBT community that had not before been identified as a potent political force was seniors. Liz Malia:

Seniors really responded to the same-sex marriage issue. One of the things that I believe moved people was the organizing that went on to reach out to those who provide elder services and in talking about the older community of LGBT people, what those issues meant for them, in terms of their own welfare and ability to thrive.

A director of one of the home-care advocacy groups in Boston got together with others to start a lesbian and gay aging project. They were able to work with a significant number of care providers, folks working in the social service mode, and found that in fact there was a significant population, that it was very hard to identify, and that some issues, such as isolation, depression, and health in general, were issues that really affected them. The aging project folks went out and did a lot of talking to senior centers, providers, anybody who would listen. They said, "Hey, there's a population that you serve, or that you're a part of, who have these issues. It can be frightening and horribly isolating. What can you do about that? Do you want to do something about that?"

Aside from the fact that the early years of the debate were mostly focused on LGBT people having kids and families, which took up a lot of the emotional focus, I think this was the balancing piece that finally got a lot of folks to the point where they could say, "It's not just about a self-identified, select group of people who are activists. This really is something that crosses all boundaries in terms of race, class, ethnic background, cultural background."

This made a major impact, I think, in terms of sending the older gay and lesbian people who felt comfortable in being out to their legislators – not just in urban areas, not just in Provincetown and Boston and wherever those of us who are likely suspects might be found – but in the more rural and suburban parts of the state, and getting those folks to come out and say, "Hey, I'm one of your constituents, and I'm interested in this issue. I also want you to know that I'm concerned about benefits, I'm concerned about the ballot question having a very negative impact on us, and I vote and will hold you accountable for this."

Overall, this strategy tends not to be easy for many communities, because I've worked with very distinct groups like the African-American and Latino communities. It's very hard for everybody to get on the same page in agreement and move forward and share agendas. But the gay community did an incredible job in setting aside differences, in coalescing resources, and in reaching out to people.

At the same time, the opponents of same-sex marriage were actively involved in lobbying the General Court, as MFI President Ronald Crews described.

Literally thousands of people participated in the process, many for the first time in ever being involved. That was an encouragement. There were people who came in early morning and stayed until midnight with us. Then there were coalitions that came together, some folks who rarely work with each other on other issues, who came together for a common cause in a greater need.

Massachusetts Citizens for Life, for example, is an organization in the state that's always focused on pro-life issues, and they never worked with us on any other issues because they're single-cause to focus on life issues. But they saw this as a life issue. And rightly so, I believe, because of the requirement for homosexual couples to have children, the artificial insemination, and there are other issues they saw as related. So they became a full-fledged member of our coalition. And that was a real encouragement to me, because they brought some resources to the table in terms of their network of folks.

Then there were the national groups that came in to stand with us and the folks who stepped forward to help us financially at Mass Family Institute. Some of our major donors, who give us $10,000 or $15,000 a year, began to step up to the plate with gifts of $50,000. There were two gifts in particular that came just at really critical times for us, to be able to do some mass mailings we wanted to do and to print some material we wanted to print. The funds would not be there. Then a phone call would come, and a check would turn up. That was very encouraging to me, the fact that folks stepped to the plate when they needed to.

We had people from various legislative districts with whom we met and gave talking points and sessions on how to talk to legislators. That sort of thing. We encouraged them to set up meetings with their legislators. So that a state legislator would come to X coffee shop in their town or their district office and meet with six, eight, ten, sometimes twenty constituents who we had prepared to be able to talk through the issue. And that's where some legislators told those constituents one thing and then voted another, and that's what we're going to be reminding voters of in November [2004].

With substantial lobbying from both sides of the issue, the 2004 Constitutional Convention ultimately took on a life of its own. For instance, House Speaker Thomas Finneran, during a pro forma introductory greeting to the convention, surprised many legislators by proposing a constitutional amendment that read, "Only the union of one man and one woman shall be valid or recognized as a marriage in Massachusetts." The amendment lost by two votes.

The politics of political etiquette and parliamentary procedure, and not the politics of policy, caused the defeat. Philip Travis recounted the convention's opening day.

I expected to go up to debate and take the slings and arrows from the other side and perhaps have an up-or-down vote on the issue. We did have 101 votes at that point in time going into the convention. We thought it would be easy. It was not, because the first thing that happened the moment that we opened the convention and the gavel came down was that the president of the senate, Mr. Travaglini, realized that he hadn't given the speaker of the house the opportunity to say a few words of greeting. And someone should have known something was wrong, because the Speaker was not at the podium with the president. Instead, he was down sitting behind a member's desk, which made him now an active member to participate. And as he finished his brief remarks welcoming everyone and [encouraging them] to be civil and to discuss this in a tone so that everyone across the nation would understand that Massachusetts has civility in its process, he finished and then immediately walked to the president of the senate and offered him an amendment to the [pending] bill. It was something I believe he had drafted at home that weekend. It was very much what I wanted but added other language.

I voted for that further amendment because it did exactly what I'd hoped. It protected marriage fully. But he antagonized most of the people in the hall who were with me. And to the delight of those against me, it just built up a force, and we went into recess for several hours. When we came back to vote on his further amendment, we lost by two votes of getting 101. I think the vote was 98 for and 102 against. We lost the momentum. So from that point on, it actually became a catch-up game for myself. I offered further amendments to try to save the situation, and debate went on day in and day out. If we had an up-or-down vote early, we would have won. It wasn't in the making.

The speaker apparently thought he could win early in the convention, but miscalculated, as Senator Richard T. Moore further described.

[Speaker Finneran's] own supporters resented not having been brought into the discussion earlier. Some folks who vote with him on almost everything else felt miffed that they were taken by surprise. They felt they were being used as pawns in not having taken part in that decision. Even if the Speaker couldn't have spoken with his own caucus beforehand, if he had had discussions with the [Republican] minority leader, he might've gotten enough votes.

MFI's Ronald Crews saw his side's best opportunity for victory squandered.

I must say that during the first day of the Constitutional Convention, when Speaker Finneran offered his amendment, that lost by two votes, that was a surprise to us. It was a disappointment on several levels. We had met the day before with several key legislators – not the Speaker, but several key lawmakers – going over process and various amendments. We had gotten wind of the Travaglini-Lees Amendment [defining marriage as only between one man and one woman but also authorizing the creation of civil unions for same-sex couples with all the rights and responsibilities of marriage] and knew it was coming. We thought we'd developed some strategy on how we were going to handle that.

But Speaker Finneran surprised us with his motion, and quite frankly, I was very disappointed in that process. If we had known, we could've worked with him on the floor to get those other two votes. And we lost at that point. That was a significant defeat for us, and I don't know how to explain it.

Looking back over and talking with people who've worked with the Speaker for years, this was pretty much in line with the way the Speaker likes to work. He keeps things very close and makes decisions and acts [snaps his fingers]. I don't understand that. I was disappointed and shared that with him.

I believe that we could have helped him be successful if we'd been given the opportunity. We scrambled to get the votes that we got once we saw what was happening. One of his key leaders came out and explained to us what was going on, and we started working the floor to get people released from a hard-line nothing-but-the-Phil-Travis-amendment [which also banned all benefits to same-sex couples] and get our votes over there to him.

But it just wasn't there. A few people later told us that they voted with great regret against that. They voted out of concern for the procedure and not the content, and based on subsequent events, regretted their vote. They apologized to us for voting against it. If they had known the consequences down the road, they would have voted with the Speaker.

[We weren't able to regroup after that], and I don't fully know [why]. We were disappointed in several legislators who we thought would be with us on some votes that turned out not to be. And it seemed like every vote from then on had its own uniqueness of folks who were with us but may have voted against us for some other reason. And it was a different category of four or five legislators at each point, that if we'd gotten them all on record at the same time, we could've gotten something passed. But it didn't happen.

But I have to begrudgingly tip my hat to [Senate President] Travaglini, who pretty much knew from the outset what he wanted the outcome to be. Again, the authority of the senate president, who holds the gavel, and therefore controls the flow of the convention and when votes are going to be and what votes will be – he was successful in accomplishing what he wanted. And that was a major disappointment for us. I am grateful that he told me personally that he would not do a Tom Birmingham and would allow a vote. So he honored that and did give us a vote. However, he was successful, and we were not.

The other major disappointment was Brian Lees, the Republican minority leader in the Senate, who bucked the governor and his Republican colleagues and worked primarily with Travaglini rather than the Republican caucus. If he had come over to help us, and he never did, then the outcome could've been different.

Indeed, during the four days of the Constitutional Convention spread out over two months, the political balance tipped from an outright ban of same-sex marriage to the Travaglini-Lees Amendment, which passed in March by a vote of 105 to 92 and would create a legal entity for same-sex couples having all the attributes of marriage except the name. Representative Peisch, who hadn't before given much notice to same-sex marriage, described the evolution of her thought on the subject.

The matter that was before us [at the Constitutional Convention] was a proposed constitutional amendment that would limit the definition of marriage to one man and one woman. I was against that. To me, that was very discriminatory. I was concerned that not only would it restrict the rights of homosexual couples but possibly any single parent, for example. I thought it was very broadly written, and had some language about no rights or benefits of marriage could inure to anyone who did not fit the definition. I imagined that that could be interpreted to restrict all kinds of rights way beyond the simple objective that the proponents claimed to be pursuing.

There was lots of discussion as to what was the appropriate position to take on the issue. There was great fear that that particular amendment might pass because of what we were all hearing from our constituents about their dissatisfaction with the court's opinion. The campaign being waged by those who were very much opposed to the concept of marriage [for same-sex couples] was focusing on allowing the people to have a voice in the matter – which is a very difficult argument to respond to because to disagree with it suggests that one thinks that your constituents are incapable of making this decision. We come across as being arrogant.

Five days before the convention, I still thought the civil union concept made the most sense. And I was leaning toward supporting that. But the discussion was constant. I was hearing from lots of my constituents, on both sides of the question, and clearly hearing from a lot of the advocates. I reread the court's decision and read the advisory opinion on the question. But what I finally realized is that the only amendment that I would consider supporting would be one that would confer every single right and benefit that marriage would confer. So then I thought, if it's everything but the name, what's the problem?

And I realized it had a lot to do with one's level of comfort. This was a concept that was foreign to most of us. It was a little uncomfortable to think of marriage as something different from what I had grown up with. When I really thought about it in those terms, I decided that I couldn't vote to amend the constitution just because I felt a little uncomfortable or my constituents felt a little uncomfortable.

Time was on the side of same-sex marriage advocates during the Constitutional Convention. Alice Hanlon Peisch:

[There was an advantage] to having the Constitutional Convention go on as long as it did. That was something I did not anticipate.

I actually thought the longer it dragged on, the worse the whole situation would get politically. Two things surprised me.

One was the level of debate, which was extraordinary, and not something you see a lot of around here on any issue. I'd be surprised if this is significantly different from any other legislature. Most of the time when we're considering legislation, most of us know way ahead of time what our position is on it. People get up and make speeches, but the speeches are directed at outside the building. There's not a whole lot of attention being paid by the members as to what's going on at the podium.

But on this issue, I'd say there were a fair number of people who were not sure, when it started, where they were going to end up. And there were people who listened to the debate and changed their minds.

And I think the same thing happened in the general public. The immediate reaction of a lot of people was, this is a little peculiar. They didn't think they liked it. But when forced to deal with it and think about, many people I think came to appreciate that this was the right thing to do.

A further explanation for the ConCon's failure to overturn the *Goodridge* decision completely is that religious conservatives, especially the Commonwealth's Roman Catholic leadership, may have overplayed their hand in the controversy, as Liz Malia clarified.

[The same-sex marriage debate] is one of the first times I've ever seen the conservative Catholics get in bed with fundamentalists and people who in any other place in this country hate Catholics. It was really interesting to see some of the alliances that developed.

[In addition, t]he role of the Massachusetts [child] abuse scandal is interesting to ponder here. It undermines some of the church's pre-existing authority. There's an awful lot of anger [out there]. Part of my district the last two years has been more Catholic and conservative than I've had before. And I'm amazed at the amount of support we got from some of those folks who had a lot of anger [at the Church] for the first time in their lives.

It's been a very emotional, traumatic event for them, questioning what happened during all of this abuse. And as more and more of that came out, people seemed to really lose faith and confidence and be very angry at what happened to them, feeling that they were getting something other than the truth about what went on and that they were being used.

This was a flashpoint for a lot of folks. Just hearing anecdotes from people, sort of working-class white folks, saying, "You know, who the hell are these priests? Who the hell are these guys to tell me anything?" – this from people who would not necessarily have focused on the issue one way or another, and certainly would not have looked at it sympathetically. If nothing else, they weren't going to fight for the Church. They weren't going to answer its rallying cry to lobby and push.

Alice Hanlon Peisch was also critical of religious leaders.

The way the Catholic Church behaved in this situation was shocking to me, and by Catholic Church, I mean its hierarchy. That they would spend the amount of time, money, and energy that they did to advocate against treating people equally is quite disturbing to me.

Some of the demonstrators who were against gay marriage were vicious. The e-mails that we received from across the country [were of the variety] "You're going to burn in hell!" But the Archbishop stood up on the podium with people making the most cruel statements. He claimed that he wasn't in favor of those tactics, but that didn't prevent him from getting on the stage with the people who were spouting this awful stuff.

I don't agree with the Church's position on abortion, but I understand it. If one believes that it is murder, I can understand how one would feel the need to be against it. But the Church didn't put anywhere near the time and energy into the anti-abortion movement that they did on this.

When you consider the abuse cases here and the Cardinal's handling of them, I just find it astonishing that the Church chose to take such a high profile and mean-spirited stand on this subject.

Some lawmakers immediately felt the political heat that their speeches generated. Senator Moore related what happened to a colleague who said same-sex marriage was a civil rights issue.

Probably one of the most fascinating aspects of the debate was that a lot of [the floor speeches] centered around its being a civil rights issue, with the feeling that people of the same sex have some constitutional or basic right to marry. The office next to mine belongs to Senator Dianne Wilkerson, our only African-American member, who is from Boston. I came into work one morning, and there were probably about twenty black clergymen standing outside her office talking with her in rather animated form. They were very upset with her because she had voted, in effect, for same-sex marriage. They were telling her it wasn't a civil rights issue in their opinion. They knew civil rights, and this was not one of them. It was fascinating just to hear that discussion.

African-American legislators weren't the only ones seeing similarity with the civil rights movement. Alice Hanlon Peisch:

I think initially that when it was described as a civil rights issue, I thought the piece about the rights and benefits I could see as having some civil rights claim to it. But I wasn't so sure that marriage really was a civil right to which everyone was entitled.

Then I came to appreciate that it is. I think the difference is that people who are discriminated against on the basis of their skin color, it's pretty obvious right off the bat what the issue is. Whereas I don't happen to believe that homosexuality is a choice, as some people say. If you believe it's a choice, then you don't see this as a civil rights issue, because you think you can just choose to do something else.

But I don't think that's the case. If you think about some of the horrific things that happen to gay people [such as Matthew Shepard] who are murdered. That's just like lynchings as far as I can tell. So I think there are a lot of similarities. It just isn't quite as obvious.

Several lawmakers characterized the 2004 ConCon as the only time in recent memory when the legislature conducted itself in a truly deliberative manner. Liz Malia:

It's hard to describe how emotional and intense it was until you've seen some of those speeches in the convention. Some people are not known for being big orators or not debating very much.

Legislators are in different groups. People who always have an opinion are always up at the podium. Other folks very seldom speak except when they have something very specific to them.

But the amount of participation at that convention was *just* . . . I still think back about some of the speeches. One individual, Kathi-Anne Reinstein, who's a rep from Revere – which is more of an older, working-class, ethnic neighborhood, more hardscrabble, definitely more conservative and Catholic – she gave an incredible speech. "I'm from Revere. People look at me and say, 'You're from Revere,' and they don't expect anything of me. They think I'm going to be less than others. So I identify with gay people." She really did.

So many people were sympathetic with some part of what happens to gay folk. The majority leader of the house, Sal DiMasi, got up and talked about growing up poor in the North End, in a cold water flat, in the Italian neighborhood there, and remembered being picked on because he was Italian.

Many who really identified with us have been bullied on some level. A lot of folks who were finally able to see this said, "What's the big deal? I know this person, and I don't really care." So there were significant shifts and some real leadership that happened. Once the ball got rolling, there was no stopping it. There was a lot of soul-bearing that went on.

They were just people, not all stars. A lot of them just spoke their hearts. It was very genuine. And I think that helped us.

David Paul Linsky reinforced the assessment that the 2004 Constitutional Convention represented a deliberative process that is rare in legislatures.

Overall, it was an experience beyond belief. It's hard to imagine that any other moment in my legislative career could be more emotional or involved than what we went through during the Constitutional Convention. This was a highlight. It really was.

There were a number of my colleagues who shared incredibly personal experiences. My colleagues on both sides of this issue clearly rose to the occasion. They gave more thought and attention to this issue than I could ever imagine giving to any other. It was truly a wonderful experience.

I distinctly remember the strategy sessions that we had several times a day, either at the Unitarian Universalist center that's next to the statehouse or in statehouse conference rooms, figuring out every little parliamentary minutiae in various permutations. We were extraordinarily well prepared. For me, it was much like gearing up for murder cases as a prosecutor. You need to be unbelievably overprepared regarding every simple fact, anticipating the last possible thing that could happen during the course of a trial. It was the same type of intensity at the ConCon. And the difference was, rather than having one or two lawyers on either side, we had seventy-six people who were involved in this thing. It was a tremendous experience.

Also, there were no throwaway votes. Everybody took every single vote, procedural or substantive, incredibly seriously. We wrestled with what the right vote was to be, every single one. We rose to a new high. We really did.

Representative Malia emphasized the institutional dynamic that evolved in the General Court during the Constitutional Convention.

[The legislative experience with same-sex marriage] threw off a lot of the negative stereotypes that many of us [lawmakers] labor under. And it was one issue where *I* felt comfortable going to the opposition and saying, "Look, we've all been criticized up here for not having any guts, and going along to get along, and not defining our own status and positions on policy issues." This was where that process clearly happened. And it happened publicly. There were a lot of meetings with other legislators that were pretty much open strategy sessions. We had great fights that come with the territory.

It's a sign of a healthy legislative process, when you can do that, have those issues, get them out in the open, do the back-and-forth, and then agree. People come to the compromise and stay focused, get organized, and move forward together.

And you could go back to the opponents, and to some of the conservatives who were attacking us by saying that the courts did this, and say, "Actually, in fact, the legislature really did its job in this case."

Even MFI's Ronald Crews, who was far from satisfied with the ConCon's hybrid outcome (the Travaglini-Lees Amendment), acknowledged that the lawmakers did their job.

We were concerned the very first day of the convention, because there were nine items on the calendar, and the marriage issue was number eight on the list. Many of us were concerned that they would just go through the motions and never get around to number eight. But we and others asked for [a change], and the [senate] president, under his full authority, just moved item eight to number one. I was surprised and very pleased and grateful for that. I think the legislators realized that they weren't able to hide from this issue. When you've got 5,000 people packed into the statehouse, so much so that the guards even had to close the doors, leaving other people outside – the lawmakers had to deal with the issue.

There was opportunity then for debate. Some of us were disappointed by the initial speeches by folks on our side. We didn't feel that they were as prepared as they could have been. There was more emotion than facts and substance. We tried to work with them, and so in the next two meetings, they had materials and talking points. In that sense, there was the opportunity for people to say what they wanted on the subject. And there were numerous votes, some procedural, some substantive. In that sense, they did [their job]. It was deliberative.

Moreover, the process was civil, as Representative Travis recognized: "[In 2002,] there were people marching in front of homes with placards, which was very ugly. We converted it to a civil process [in 2004]. It was noisy in the building, don't misunderstand. Both sides were shouting to the top of their voices. But no one raised a fist or pulled another person's sign down."

The Legislative Debates

As noted, the arguments over same-sex marriage among legislators during the 2004 Massachusetts Constitutional Convention were an extraordinary example of the deliberative lawmaking process at its best. Excerpts from those speeches in the Boston statehouse are offered here.

Several important themes emerged, one of the most prominent of which was foreshadowed by the "Let the people vote!" chants of spectators at the close of the truncated 2002 ConCon. In February and March 2004, Massachusetts state senators and representatives agonized over whether to send a ballot question on same-sex marriage to the people of the Commonwealth, as these samples from the legislative debates indicate:

Senator **Brian Lees**: [The Travaglini-Lees Amendment] allows this issue to move forward and [to] put something on the ballot. ... [We] have worked very hard to ensure the [people's] voices are heard and we have something on the ballot .... It would be a sad day to leave here without having something on the ballot. We have heard from the people that they want to be heard on this issue. ... Somehow we are going to get a ballot question. It is going to happen.

Senator **Brian Joyce**: Polls show the argument to let the people decide has great appeal. ... We [legislators] are charged with exercising our judgment. It is our responsibility to cast votes, even when the matter is controversial. ... I am unconvinced that civil rights should be decided [at] the ballot box when emotions are so inflamed. Had the ban on interracial marriage or the decision [de]segregating schools been put on the ballot, each may have been overturned. That does not mean those decisions were wrong.

Representative **Philip Travis**: In this dilemma we have, it is the outside people who want the right to vote. It is the people inside [the statehouse] who have to grant them that right. My vote is not more important than theirs. No. Not on an issue of this magnitude.

Senator **Bruce Tarr**: For me, one of the reasons this has been such an incredibly difficult issue is that we have two different spheres clashing in front of us: the right to vote, and the right that people are equal and should have the right to join together in associations without the interference of the state. ... Is it our obligation to put something on the ballot? Proudly, we have proven that is not our obligation. Unlike some of what has been said, I disagree that the voters will always do the wrong thing. I think, more often than not, the voters do the right thing. ... This amendment finds an accommodation as close to one that can be found. There will never be anything closer, but it says we value the right for the people to vote.

Representative **Paul Demakis**: [Senator Lees] expressed a view that we needed to put something on the ballot. He said this is what the people wanted. I disagree. We have seen a legislature that is deeply, deeply divided. We had a two-vote margin [in this convention], [then] a ten-vote margin, and an eleven-vote margin. We are a reflection of the people who sent us here. If we are so evenly divided, we can be sure that they are, too. If you look at the numbers in the polls, it shows a deeply divided electorate. Half may want to vote on this, [and the other half] wants to accept the SJC decision. When we have such a deeply divided electorate on a question of this magnitude, we ought not to take the risk that on a very, very narrow majority we enshrine an amendment in the constitution that has nearly half the people against it. ...

The split in public opinion on these issues is generational. Older voters vote overwhelmingly against extending rights to gays and lesbians. Contemplate the possibility that we could put this on the ballot and have it decided by a tiny majority and have a situation in five to ten years that we have a clear majority against it, and we have to go through the cumbersome process of changing the constitution to bring it back in line with public opinion.

Senator **Cynthia Creem:** We are talking about equality, and that is why we should not put this on the ballot. This is not a tax matter for the ballot. This is about rights. Gays have suffered oppression and hate. We should not send a measure restricting the rights of the few for the whim of the majority. We may appeal to every page of history to see that the people can be just as barbarous as any king possessed of power. Popular votes are no way to protect fundamental rights. ... As a Jewish person, I fully understand the need to protect minorities. I am very happy not to have my rights subject to a statewide vote.

Another topic arising in the legislative debates centered on the definition of marriage, as reflected in this exchange:

Representative **David Flynn:** This is not about religion. It's not about a bible. It's not about civil rights. It's not about civil law. It's about natural law with me, the law of nature. The Supreme Judicial Court can and does invoke the law of man. The Supreme Judicial Court cannot repeal the law of nature. I support traditional marriage and civil unions. Representative **Ruth Balser:** I would never limit in our constitution a definition of marriage that excludes loving couples. I have heard that, for millennia, marriage has been the union of one man and one woman. Jewish people have been persecuted for thousands of years. I doubt that anyone here would say we should continue that millennial practice. It is not hard to think of other examples. For millennia, women have been forced to be subjugated to men in many areas of the globe. But the fact that something has been so for many years does not mean we are not free to alter it.

A third leitmotif of the 2004 ConCon was the appropriate roles of the legislature and courts in public policy making.

Representative **Eugene O'Flaherty:** The legislature is the proper place to make public policy, not the supreme court. Every one of you should be personally insulted that the court has said, "Close your doors as legislators. We are going to decide what's public policy."
Representative **Cory Atkins:** I am insulted by the words about the courts. The courts did not ask for this legislation or reach out to the public. It went there because of inaction of the House. ... The courts interpret the constitution. That is their job. We could have had the opportunity to vote on this in various forms many times before today. It never ever had to come to this crisis.

The final important theme in the legislative debates was whether gay people's fight for marriage rights is a bona fide civil rights claim. Note that the first three speeches here are by African-American lawmakers:

Senator **Dianne Wilkerson:** One group of citizens cannot be almost equal to the others. I was born not far from Little Rock. ... My parents are from Arkansas. My grandparents all lived in segregated southern Arkansas. I was but one generation removed from an existence in slavery. And to this day I carry the name of that dark and ugly history of being almost equal. Slaves were given the names of their masters. The names end in "son." It signifies ownership. It is with that knowledge and history that I [approach] the question today. Through my lens, the picture could not be more clear. ... Simply put, this is a civil rights matter. It should not be left to the public to be decided by popular vote. I represent many of those affected by this decision. They feel, they care, they love, and they are deserving. This is a civil rights issue.
This week I witnessed a group of persons announce a position contrary to my own. The black clergy in my darkest moment embraced

me and got me through a tough time. I understand and respect the[ir] position but respectfully disagree.

I have filed [bills for] domestic partnerships each and every year for six terms. It was a morally correct effort to engage. It has been made moot by the rulings of the court. Domestic partnership protection would still reflect less than equal. This is why I cannot support the civil union option. ... I am not sure how anyone can advocate for a status that leaves people less than equal. I can't and won't turn back now. Protection of rights must include the extension of the most basic of civil rights, the right to marry.

I was born in my grandmother's house in a shotgun shack in Arkansas. The public hospital did not allow blacks to deliver children [there]. We lived in constant fear of the Ku Klux Klan. Blacks had to pull off the road for whites to pass. I had two uncles that decided enough was enough in 1935. It cost them thirty years of their lives. It sent one uncle to Springfield, which is how I got there. I can't send anyone to that place from where my family fled. My grandmother would never forgive me.

Representative **Marie St. Fleur:** You can't compromise on discrimination. You can't color it another way. Let's start with race. You have to deal with it. We had to deal with it in the constitution, with women and immigrants. I, my friends, fit all those categories, and but for the equal protection of the laws, I would not enjoy the position and freedom I enjoy today. I cannot compromise on the constitution. I can't compromise on discrimination. I am also Catholic. But I cannot say "yes" to [a DOMA]. My role as a legislator is separate from my role in a parish. But we are seeking state action here – not private action, not religious action. And if the state is involved in marriage, we ought to do it equally. That's one of the fundamental protections of government. ... What is special about this American democracy is we are willing to put aside the power of the majority to respect the power of the minority. This is not simply about gay rights. This is about who we are as an American democracy.

Representative **Benjamin Swan:** Through tenth grade, I experienced separate but equal. My school received hand-me-down football equipment. ... I hope my experience provides a frame of experience. Listeners can understand how it feels to be designated as different from the majority. I entered the military in 1953 and witnessed the painted-over "colored only" signs. I traveled in integrated and segregated buses. ...

People wonder, "Why associate the struggle of gays and lesbians with the struggle of blacks in America?" I thought about that. I helped organize the March on Washington. I was in Alabama before and after the march. I worked for the civil rights law that was passed in 1964. Yes, it's about civil rights. Anytime two people come before the law and they do not have the same rights, something is wrong with that. If any two people come before me, and I deal with them differently under the law, then something is wrong with that. We are talking about civil rights. It is about civil rights.

I have had discussions with family members. I am one of fifteen children, the eleventh child of George and Sally Swan, and some of my brothers disagree with me. I asked my brother a few days ago, if it's not discrimination and it's not about civil rights, then why do I hear the same words I heard when people opposed children going to school together or access by all to public accommodations or about buses being integrated? Representative **Marie Parente**: We have been characterized as antigay, anticolor, anti-Semitic. Let me tell you about color. I talked to a woman of color, and she told me, "You don't get it." I said, "Italians were discriminated against in Milford." She said, "You don't get it. If people just see you, they won't know you are Catholic or Italian. But when I walk into a room, people know." So don't compare this to other movements. Representative **Steven Walsh**: In the twentieth century, this commonwealth was a leader in supporting the rights of women. Imagine that, back then, not a single seat in this chamber was occupied by a woman. This is not a time for blacks, not a time for women. It's a time for gays.

I was out to dinner last Friday night. The waiter recognized me and said, "I'm gay. But is it my choice to be gay? Is it my choice to be beaten, to be laughed at, to be spit at? Who would choose this?" he said. "This is how God created me." Because of their skin color or their religion, many people in this room have been discriminated against. In the twenty-first century, this state is asking to lead another revolution. ... Unlike the budget, where funding one program leaves another one unfunded, granting rights to one group does not take it away from another. It just extends the circle.

Aftermath

In interviews before the 2004 Massachusetts primary and general elections, both sides of the same-sex marriage controversy had the

2000 Vermont model in mind and expected that voters might indirectly resolve the marriage issue in legislative races. Liz Malia:

> Maybe this is wishful thinking on our part, but some think that if this [2004] weren't an election year, we really would've been able to put this issue to sleep. Our success will depend upon how well we do in this election cycle. Are we able to protect those folks with conservative constituencies who really went out on a limb for us? Can we keep them in the legislature? Maybe we pick up some new blood. This election cycle is going to be really interesting in terms of where we go next.

MassEquality's Marty Rouse put the matter more forcefully.

> Our job right now is to make sure our supporters vote to protect our incumbents in trouble in primaries and then defend them in the general election as well. So it's very clear to my mind what we need to do. I would be shocked if any incumbent loses on same-sex marriage, because they're campaigning door to door, and this isn't coming up as an issue.
>
> In fact, we're working extremely hard at MassEquality to knock out some antigay incumbents in the primaries. Plus we need to defend two incumbents with serious challengers. Our overarching goal is to protect every incumbent who voted with us. We want to make sure we don't have a net loss.
>
> But what we really want is a net gain. I would be thrilled if we could pick up one, two, or even three seats. If we can hold our own, that sends a signal, because that takes care of the Vermont model.

MFI's Ronald Crews also awaited the 2004 elections and made his own prediction: "I do believe there is the potential for a ten- to fifteen-seat turnaround [in the General Court], which for this state is pretty significant."

In the September 2004 Massachusetts primary, all seven same-sex marriage supporters in the legislature who faced challengers for their party's nomination in fact won. Moreover, two Democratic incumbents who opposed marriage for same-sex couples lost to rivals who favored it. One of the upsets was a David-versus-Goliath story (Lewis 2004). Vincent Ciampa was a sixteen-year Democratic incumbent from Somerville who served as a lieutenant to Speaker Finneran and who opposed both same-sex marriage and civil unions. Somerville's popular young mayor, Joseph Curtatone, and the rest of the city's political establishment endorsed Ciampa in the Democratic primary. Carl Sciortino, a twenty-seven-year-old gay man who never before held political office, challenged Ciampa. With the help of SupportEquality.org (a Web site steering financial donations to Massachusetts legislative candidates supporting same-sex marriage) and numerous grass-roots volunteers motivated by the marriage issue, Sciortino won the election in a close vote.

In the November general election, all fifty incumbent Massachusetts legislators who faced challengers and who opposed a constitutional amendment banning same-sex marriage won reelection. At the same time, in four open seats, departing lawmakers who championed the *Goodridge* outcome were replaced with like-minded successors. In another five open races where retiring office holders had opposed same-sex marriage, three seats were filled with supporters. Thus, the 2004 election cycle produced a net gain of five supporters in the legislative same-sex marriage calculus. Moreover, in three special elections for state representative in March and April of 2005, legislators who opposed same-sex marriage were replaced with *Goodridge* supporters.

Especially important to the legislative-vote reckoning was the large psychological impact that Massachusetts's negating the Vermont model brought. Several lawmakers said they knew of colleagues who would have backed *Goodridge* in March 2004 but didn't out of fear of constituent reprisal.

Representative Malia raised a second important political variable in the legislative equation: "It depends upon who our leadership is, if there's any change there. That's one possibility that gets talked about. It's out there for a number of reasons."

Malia was prescient, because Speaker Thomas Finneran, who vigorously opposed *Goodridge* and supported Ciampa's failed reelection bid, resigned less than two weeks after the primary. Equally important, House Majority Leader Salvatore DiMasi, a strong supporter of same-sex marriage, succeeded Finneran as Speaker. As the *Boston Globe* reported:

> The effort to bring a constitutional amendment banning gay marriage to voters in November 2006 suffered a major setback [with the departure of Finneran and elevation of DiMasi].
>
> A key legislative backer of the proposed amendment to ban same-sex marriage and establish civil unions all but declared defeat, saying that Finneran's exit from Beacon Hill was the final straw in an effort that already was in trouble because the state has legalized same-sex marriage with little of the uproar predicted by opponents.
>
> "It is pretty much over," said Senate Minority Leader Brian Lees. (Phillips 2004)

With this leadership change and the net gain of eight votes among same-sex marriage supporters in the General Court between September 2004 and August 2005, the September 2005 ConCon rejected the Travaglini-Lees Amendment by an overwhelming margin: 157 to 39. Even Republican co-author Brian Lees voted against it, stating, "Gay marriage has begun, and life has not changed for the citizens of the Commonwealth, with the exception of those who can now marry. This amendment, which was an appropriate measure or compromise a year ago, is no longer, I feel, a compromise today" (LeBlanc 2005).

Yet Massachusetts's struggle for same-sex marriage isn't necessarily over, as Representative Linsky made clear:

> What I fear is a citizens' initiative that would be a strict ban on same-sex marriage with no civil unions component. That requires about 120,000 signatures and only fifty votes (25 percent) in two successive constitutional conventions to move forward. That's not an unlikely scenario. I think there are enough activists out there who could get the 120,000 signatures within a matter of days if they needed to.

Marty Rouse of MassEquality echoed Linsky's expectation.

If we do win in the legislature in 2005, then there will probably be a citizen petition by our opponents. That's what they ultimately want anyway, because they're not happy with a compromise enshrining civil unions in the state constitution. They'll try to rewrite the constitution to say one man and one woman and not mention civil unions at all and put that to the voters in 2008. So I'm fairly confident if we don't confront a ballot measure in 2006, we're definitely facing one in 2008.

This issue is just like abortion. It's not going away. It will keep coming up in different ways. They're not going to let it be.

Indeed, Kris Mineau, the new president of the Massachusetts Family Institute, declared that his organization would launch a signature drive the week after the 2005 ConCon for a citizen initiative banning same-sex marriage and not mentioning civil unions. If enough signatures are secured, and if 25 percent of legislators in two successive constitutional conventions approve the measure, then the referendum would appear on the 2008 ballot (LeBlanc 2005).

Representative Philip Travis emphasized the fervor of opposition to same-sex marriage in the Bay State.

We all want to give people the rights to have insurance and to transfer property. No one is so rotten to the core that they wouldn't even consider that. That would be inappropriate.

But we don't want to call it marriage. And remember, *they* held out for marriage. Civil unions weren't acceptable to the gay community in Massachusetts. They didn't want a second-sister relationship like they have in Vermont. They wanted the full-blown description with the title of marriage.

Protecting marriage is the most important position a politician or public servant has to take. If you decimate the family unit in the United States, it's the beginning of the end of our nation as a country that's, not owing to God for its creation, but saying, "In God we trust." We'll be nothing if we don't protect the family unit that's been basically the same for five thousand years. It's the beginning of the downfall of America. I think the moral fabric of the United States will falter so badly that other peoples will have total disrespect for us. And I don't want that happening while I'm in office.

FOUR

California

THE STATE OF CALIFORNIA has been a leader in the legal recognition of relationship rights. In 1948, the California Supreme Court was the first court of last resort to strike down a state prohibition on interracial marriage (*Perez v. Sharp*), nineteen years before the U.S. Supreme Court nullified all such bans in *Loving v. Virginia* (1967). In 1982, San Francisco's city council, called the Board of Supervisors, passed the nation's first domestic partnership ordinance, authored by gay supervisor Harry Britt and vetoed by then Mayor Diane Feinstein. A 1990 voter initiative, also prompted by Britt, amended San Francisco's Administrative Code to recognize domestic partnerships. In 1996, under the leadership of gay supervisors Tom Ammiano and Leslie Katz, San Francisco enacted the nation's first equal benefits ordinance, requiring all private companies that contract with the city or county to offer the same benefits to the same-sex partners of their employees that they offer to the spouses of their employees. Most consequentially for lesbian and gay Californians, by 2003, the state legislature, at the behest of two lesbian lawmakers, Assemblywoman Jackie Goldberg and Senator Carole Migden, granted domestic partners all state-conferred rights of marriage but for two (filing as married couples on state income tax returns, and having earned income considered as couples' community property). Thus, California first created full civil union benefits for same-sex couples by legislative action not prompted by court intervention.

Yet the most notorious California "first" in relationship rights was San Francisco Mayor Gavin Newsom's decision, announced on February 12, 2004, to instruct the San Francisco County Clerk to issue marriage licenses to same-sex couples. Phyllis Lyon and Del Martin, together for fifty-one years and the founders, in 1955, of the first national lesbian organization, the Daughters of Bilitis, were the first same-sex couple to receive a marriage license under Mayor Newsom's directive. On March 11, the California Supreme Court ordered San Francisco to cease issuing marriage licenses to lesbian and gay couples. During the twenty-nine-day "Month of Marriages" or "Winter of Love," as the time is variously called in the Bay Area, 4,037 same-sex couples received marriage licenses. In August 2004, the California Supreme Court voided those marriages, holding that Mayor Newsom and other city and county officials exceeded their authority in issuing the licenses to same-sex couples when the California Family Code defined marriage as "a personal relation arising out of a civil contract between a man and a woman" (*Lockyer v. City and County of San Francisco*).

Mayor Newsom

Gavin Newsom had been mayor for barely a month when he made his decision on same-sex marriage. Between 1997 and 2004, Newsom served on San Francisco's Board of Supervisors. He was endorsed by the Democratic Party in the 2003 mayoral race and, in December, won with 53 percent of the vote in a hotly contested match with Supervisor Matt Gonzalez, endorsed by the Green Party. Newsom was sworn into office on January 8, 2004.

The immediate catalyst for the mayor's action on same-sex marriage was the 2004 State of the Union address by President George W. Bush, delivered on January 20. Newsom was in Washington for a meeting of the U.S. Conference of Mayors and attended the speech at the invitation of Congresswoman Nancy Pelosi, the Democratic leader in the U.S. House of Representatives whose congressional district includes most of San Francisco. In the address to Congress, President Bush said:

A strong America must ... value the institution of marriage. I believe we should respect individuals as we take a principled stand for one of the most fundamental, enduring institutions of our civilization. Congress has already taken a stand on this issue by passing the Defense of Marriage Act, signed in 1996 by President Clinton. That statute protects marriage under federal law as a union of a man and a woman, and declares that one state may not redefine marriage for other states.

Activist judges, however, have begun redefining marriage by court order, without regard for the will of the people and their elected representatives. On an issue of such great consequence, the people's voice must be heard. If judges insist on forcing their arbitrary will upon the people, the only alternative left to the people would be the constitutional process. Our nation must defend the sanctity of marriage.

The outcome of this debate is important – and so is the way we conduct it. The same moral tradition that defines marriage also teaches that each individual has dignity and value in God's sight.

Although Gavin Newsom was not available to be interviewed for this book, Steve Kawa, his chief of staff, described the mayor's reaction to the Bush speech.

Mayor Newsom was in disbelief that the President of the United States brought up this issue to divide Americans and to promote discrimination. I talked to the mayor that night, because we knew the local media would want to know his reaction to the State of the Union. The mayor said we had to do something. We put out a press statement the next day.

The mayor's incredulity that this was actually happening in America caused him to think about the issue for several weeks. Then he called me into his office one day and told me he wanted us to issue same-sex, nondiscriminatory marriage licenses.

One would expect that I, as a gay man in a family with two small kids, would think that would be great. But my first reaction was "What?!" I had to think about all of the implications for my boss.

Yet the mayor is one of those rare people in life who have great instinct. On this, his instinct and belief system were one in the same. He just said, "We're going to do this. Figure out how. I took this office with an oath to uphold the Constitution of the

United States and the constitution of the state of California. I
believe in those constitutions with their equal protection clauses.
I'm not allowed to discriminate." So he signed a letter to the
County Clerk that day to look into issuing these marriage licenses.

Kate Kendell, the Executive Director of the National Center for
Lesbian Rights (NCLR), a legal advocacy organization headquartered
in San Francisco, was one of the first people outside City Hall to learn
of Mayor Newsom's action.

Forget "Where were you when JFK was shot?" For me, it's
"When did you find out about Gavin Newsom's decision to marry
lesbian and gay couples?" It was Friday, February 6, about three
o'clock in the afternoon. I was picking up my son outside his
school. My cell phone rang, and it was Steve Kawa, Mayor
Newsom's chief of staff. I had met Steve only once or twice.
I hardly knew him. And I didn't know the mayor at all. I'd never
met him. Steve said, "Kate, I'm calling to tell you that the mayor is
going to begin issuing marriage licenses to lesbian and gay couples
on Monday morning."

I was shocked and immediately went into my nervous, lay-of-
the-land, community-legal-advocate mode and started expressing
reservations about the idea. What about the folks in Massachusetts and our colleagues there? Is this going to help them? Or is it
going to increase the firestorm that they're facing? This was only
three months after the Massachusetts Supreme Judicial Court had
ruled that, yes, you had to begin issuing marriage licenses to same-
sex couples. But licenses hadn't been issued yet. So I said, "Steve,
we've really got to check this out in Massachusetts. In addition,
we've got the whole Federal Marriage Amendment situation. You
really need to think about this a little bit more. I appreciate the
mayor's sentiment and gesture."

At NCLR, we had had very preliminary discussions in the office
about approaching the mayor. It was just like sitting around the
conference table, BS-ing. We had never even connected the dots
about whether we thought it was a good idea. So I was sympathetic, obviously, but very nervous about the lay of the land.

After I finished my whole I-don't-know-I-don't-know routine,
Steve said, "Kate, that's great. But let me just be clear. On

Monday morning, the Mayor *is* going to begin issuing marriage licenses to gay and lesbian couples." The telephone call was an act of notification, not consultation.

But things did start to calm down a little bit from that point. We had a lot of conversations over the weekend, with folks at GLAD and elsewhere. The Massachusetts people were like, "Please, please, please, do it. We love the idea." They were most enthusiastic about it, because being the only place where this issue was seriously contested created enormous pressure on their legislature and on the system there to do the right thing. They liked the idea of a Western front opening up, so that there would be more of a national conversation, instead of "Massachusetts is an outlier and not part of the natural politics of the country."

On Monday morning, we met with Mayor Newsom's senior staff. Although licenses weren't issued until later that week, by Monday, I was completely convinced that we should do this. Two things were clear to me. One is that I thought it was a really good idea to ignite a national conversation. The second was that the mayor was definitely going to do it. That's the backdrop that people really need to understand. Mayor Newsom was committed to this position, absent some completely compelling reason not to, such as, "If you do this, they're going to amend the federal Constitution." Well, I couldn't say that to him. We were concerned about it, but we couldn't say that for sure.

A member of San Francisco's Board of Supervisors offered an analysis of the political calculations behind Mayor Newsom's decision.

A lot of his top senior staff are gay. His chief of staff is gay. His head of policy is gay. His head of neighborhood services is gay. So clearly that dynamic was going on there.

But more important, I think that, first, the guy felt it was right. Second, he took a calculated risk, which went as follows. The mayor had just finished a bruising election in a left-wing, gay town. He had just squeaked by with a handful of percentage points in a race that they thought would totally be his. He outspent his insurgent opponent by probably eight to one. And the city was divided. Clearly, gay marriage would go over well in San Francisco. The calculated risk was, what would it do to the rest of this ambitious mayor's political career? That answer we don't yet know. But I think what they figure is, by the time this guy is ready to be a United States senator, in a decade, will this have been Rosa Parks on the bus that the people of California are willing to accept? Stay tuned.

But clearly, it had the desired political result locally, which is that the mayor became a hero in San Francisco. The gay community was quite divided in the December mayoral contest. By March, his numbers shot up to 70 or 80 percent approval ratings, which is unheard of for a mayor of this town.

NCLR's Kate Kendell disputed this analysis.

I don't think Mayor Newsom's action in favor of marriage equality was a political choice to prop up his left after the race against Matt Gonzalez. That would have been a dumb calculation, because the mayor had as much of the left as he needed. He obviously won the election. And after doing so, he did what most progressive politicians – and certainly Democratic politicians – never do. He made a play to shore up his base, rather than abandoning that base, figuring they were going to be with him no matter what and he could go after more moderate to conservative folks. Even in this city I think that is true.

The conventional wisdom would be for him to court the moderate to conservatives and make them very happy. Because Newsom would be a more progressive candidate than virtually anyone else except a Matt Gonzalez, he'd take as much of the left as he'd need. There may always be someone who'd stake out a further position on the left, but this city is liberal, not progressive. Matt was the best chance progressives ever had. The best political minds would agree that a person further to the left would not win the mayor's seat. They're going to be on the Board of Supervisors or in other positions.

So as a political calculation, the same-sex marriage decision was not in his interest, even just considering San Francisco by itself. Furthermore, this is a guy who could be – and this remains to be seen – a candidate for higher office, maybe [U.S.] Senator [Diane] Feinstein's seat. I think he totally put that in jeopardy. Now whether he truly imperiled it, time will tell. But he certainly put that at risk in a way that was entirely unnecessary.

While I didn't know Newsom, and for all sorts of reasons had reservations about him in terms of a progressive agenda, I've come to think he's that rare sort of true believer. I have a lot of admiration and respect for him because of that.

Kendell's assessment reflected the uniform opinion about Mayor Newsom among San Francisco's lesbian and gay leadership. Molly McKay, a founder of Marriage Equality California and Associate Executive Director of Equality California, a statewide lesbian and gay organization, put it the following way.

I wholeheartedly credit Mayor Gavin Newsom with moving the issue of marriage equality a quantum leap forward. He just completely changed the world as we know it.

This was an instance like the Berlin Wall, separating gay people from straight. You don't question it. It's always been there, and makes such a difference between the two groups standing on either side. Newsom realized it was a thin wall, and just took a hammer and struck a crack in it. And as many people as could fit came rushing through that crack from the other side. For a moment, the wall began to fall, and lots of folks who thought the wall was impermeable realized it wasn't.

Newsom put same-sex couples on the radar screen of the nongay world in a way those couples had never been before. He allowed an opportunity to see real-life couples being impacted in a way that no paid-for advertising campaign or national gay and lesbian spokesperson could ever do. It was so real, and to have all of those couples wrapping around the block, standing out in the elements. ... Here you had people in their fifties and sixties waiting in line for hours in the cold and pouring rain. But they were willing to do it to make history. It gave a taste of equality to the four thousand couples who were able to marry.

It changed the nature of the debate. It wasn't something theoretical anymore. It became real. The nongay community saw something that was far from being some new social experiment. Rather, there were all these lesbian and gay couples in long-term, committed relationships, with their children, with their parents, with family there celebrating, and who'd been together at least as long as most nongay couples.

And the sky didn't fall, and the world didn't end, and we didn't see a spike in the divorce rates of heterosexual marriages.

Then when the same-sex marriages were nullified, we asked the question, "Does anyone's marriage feel more solid and more protected now that ours are invalidated?" I think it put the theory into practice. It put a face to the issue that nothing else – no legislation, no court case – could ever do.

I absolutely think it was the best thing that could have happened, especially by a heterosexual Catholic conservative. You have to realize that, by San Francisco standards, Newsom was a conservative doing this. And then to stand so resolutely in the face of the gusts and winds of opposition that came his way – to such an extent, in fact, that he's been excluded from the congregations of two Catholic churches here in San Francisco. 2004 was a hard year for the mayor. And he took the brunt of it in a way that many of us have always imagined and wished for: a big brother protecting us from schoolyard bullies. He allowed all these same-sex couples to come in and have that magic and their day.

So absolutely, Mayor Gavin Newsom is a civil rights hero. I don't think there's anybody else who could've done something more powerful, only thirty-two days in office and as a young man [thirty-seven]. He's a rising star in the Democratic Party, and history will show that he did the right thing. History will write his legacy.

The Winter of Love

Despite media predictions, California courts did not immediately end San Francisco's issuance of marriage licenses to same-sex couples. Rather, trial judges refused to grant temporary restraining orders because the Campaign for California Families and the Alliance Defense Fund, the conservative groups initially seeking to stop the marriages, failed to demonstrate irreparable injury by the further issuance of licenses. Only California Attorney General Bill Lockyer's petition to the California Supreme Court ultimately brought the judicial stay of March 11.

Nonetheless, the stoppage threat prompted gays and lesbians to rush to City Hall, so that more than three thousand couples obtained marriage licenses in the first ten days after Gavin Newsom's announcement, when fewer than a hundred opposite-sex pairs applied for licenses during the same period.

Sherri Sokeland Kaiser, a deputy city attorney for the City and County of San Francisco, characterized the response of the Bay Area's lesbian and gay community to the mayor's action.

It wasn't that much different from what a pent-up demand for, say, baptism might be. Or a pent-up demand for other really solemn occasions that mean things in people's lives, that are moments filled with deep personal significance. That was the atmosphere that pervaded the city in the days after February 12.

That time period was an incredibly memorable experience. There were just throngs of people snaking through this gorgeous building [City Hall]. The atmosphere was one of elation and love and pride as people were going into the Clerk's Office, after standing for many hours in line. The weather was bad, and people were tired, and children were fussing. But every time a couple came out of the Clerk's Office with a license, people cheered. It was just an absolutely amazing experience. And it kept up that way for the period of time when couples were allowed to wait inside the building. Whenever I left my [second-floor City Hall] office, I'd walk along the hallway bannister and see the marriage ceremonies taking place [on the first floor], and I'd hear the general hum of all these people. I literally got chills every time I walked down that hallway. It was like nothing else I've ever experienced.

I've often heard people who weren't here, largely, describe what happened in San Francisco as a spectacle or a circus. It was neither. Not at all. It was very dignified. These were people coming in with their families, having them finally recognized and being able to celebrate that. There was the pride of feeling for the first time like a full citizen, and actually being able to do this in a government building. It was a remarkably dignified process.

One of the first couples to marry was Jim and Simon, who live in San Francisco and have been together for sixteen years. Jim is forty-five and an administrator at the University of California. Simon, forty-three, is a vice president of sales and marketing for a biotech company. They described what happened following the mayor's announcement.

Jim: We were having dinner and, as always, started with a toast about something that happened that day. Simon said, "We have to toast Gavin Newsom." That really surprised me, since neither of us had voted for him and never had particularly cared for him as a politician. So I said, "What?" "Yeah, Newsom announced that he's ordered the issuance of marriage licenses to same-sex couples." I was shocked.

Simon: We were like, let's just go down to City Hall and see what happens. Let's play it by ear.

Jim: The news coverage from that day was, "This will be shut down any minute. This can't continue." So our attitude was, let's not get our hopes up. We'll show up, it'll get shut down, and we'll protest once again.

Simon: But let's not put too much store in it, so we don't get carried away.

Jim: Because we thought the opposing forces were already filing with the courts.

Simon: Little did we know then that the way it had been planned was that there was a five-day period over a holiday weekend when the courts couldn't do anything.

We decided we weren't going to be ridiculous, like get up at three o'clock in the morning. The announcement was that city offices would open at 8 A.M., so we would get there at 7 or 7:30. This is now Friday the thirteenth. When we arrived around 7:15, there were about forty or forty-five people in front of us. Like everybody else, we said we'd stand in line and see what happened. They opened the doors at 8 o'clock, and we all filed in.

Jim: Having never even considered marriage, we had no idea about what the process was, in terms of you go to this office and fill out that form.

Simon: So they instructed us on what to do. When they mentioned rings and witnesses, we thought, "Oh! We didn't think about any of this." We didn't have rings or witnesses.

The guys in line in front of us didn't have witnesses either. So, symptomatic of the emotion and camaraderie that this event fostered, we made two friends in line and were each others' witnesses. And we borrowed their rings. "Something borrowed ..."

By 10:15, it was done. We were married.

For us, City Hall has always been magical. We've both sung with the San Francisco Gay Men's Chorus in concerts in the rotunda. It's a special place. So actually having our ceremony performed on the steps of City Hall was joyous.

Jim: If I had a choice of anywhere in the city to be married, that's exactly where I'd want to go. So it was amazing that's where we got to get married.

Simon: For me, getting married was quite emotional, partly because I grew up in the United Kingdom and came here for work. Jim and I met a few months afterwards. For the first several years of our relationship, it was always, "What happens if?" I was here on student visas and then work visas. So there was always the question, if all of that fell apart, what would we do? We'd been talking about contingency plans. Fortunately, I got a green card through work and subsequently became a citizen.

But a lot of that emotion came back. Because finally, this whole thing that straight people have – and we don't – is the ability to marry a spouse who isn't a U.S. citizen and have that confer rights here. So there was that, as well as sixteen years together. I hate to say we were validated, because our relationship doesn't need validation. But there was a component of that.

Jim: For me, it was almost like an out-of-body experience. It literally was. I was in the moment, and it was incredibly emotional. Finally, after all these years, to be saying these words, these vows, to the person I love in this institution of power and know that, at least within the confines of San Francisco, this was officially blessed and certified by *all* the public officials. It just felt amazing to me.

Getting married changed the way that I see our relationship, which really, really surprised me. Our relationship *is* a marriage. Before, if I used that term, it was always with invisible quotation marks, like, oh, we're just an old "married" couple. Now I realize that I don't use that term with any sense of irony anymore. It's about being honest about what our relationship is. Neither of us ever had any idea of getting out of the relationship or seeing anything other than a future for the two of us together for the rest of our lives.

But it's one thing to feel that within yourself. It's another thing to make a public statement about it. It really changed the way that I see our relationship. As a gay man living in the year 2004 in San Francisco, I'm embarrassed to admit that I didn't see that, and that it took our straight mayor to point out a major fact of life to me. This guy I didn't even vote for, it took him saying, "You guys are married," for me to realize – *we're married*. How stupid could I have been.

Since that time, it's also made me really, really angry at the number of rights that we don't have – that we've *never* had – and that somehow before we got married, it was okay with me. I wasn't happy about it, but it was okay. I don't know what I was thinking. I guess when things are denied to you for so long, you just get used to it. I just realize now how incredibly unfair it is. I'm angry. I feel politically motivated now in a way that I never was on this issue. Even though we've been in a long-term relationship, this was never my issue.

Simon: It suddenly became that.

The Month of Marriages in San Francisco is almost indescribable. I was able to go back during that first weekend and volunteer. I wish that anyone who had concerns about this whole affair could have been there and witnessed the emotion and the joy and the absolute feeling of love that was going on.

Everybody was caught up in this emotion. I spent most of the time walking the line and helping people fill out the paperwork. It felt like, finally, someone had created this energy of absolute love and joy. And I defy anybody not to have gotten caught up in that. I don't see how anyone could not have been impacted by the raw emotion that this was causing.

There was also heartbreak. I had one situation Saturday morning. A couple from Georgia flew in that day. One of the guys had only that one day, because of business travel and other responsibilities. They were there by about two o'clock in the afternoon, by which point there were already hundreds and hundreds of people ahead of them in line. They weren't able to marry that day because they were just too far back.

When I think about our experience on Friday morning, there were only forty people in line. That was nothing. By that afternoon, there were already thousands of people, it seemed, in line. By Saturday, it was . . . . But none of that mattered.

The City Hall folks were just running by the seat of their pants. We would have to huddle from time to time with [San Francisco City Assessor-Recorder] Mabel Teng and her people and decide what to do. I don't think anybody had quite anticipated the reaction that this was going to get. But for me, it truly was one of the highlights of my life. Not just our own marriage, but also being there that weekend.

Jim: It was overwhelming. It was hard to separate ourselves from it. Once you left City Hall, part of you would still be there. You just couldn't pull yourself away from it.

Simon: It was really hard to leave.

Jim: We have some friends who are long-term partners, too. One of them was away and flew home that Sunday night. We said to them, "Look, you've got to go down." So they got up at some ridiculous hour on Monday and waited in the rain. Then we got up early and waited with them. They have kids, and we went with the kids. So we were in line for *hours* in the rain. But we couldn't not be there. We just couldn't separate ourselves. Even the whole atmosphere in the rotunda area, as marriage after marriage after marriage was going on, was sacred. It made a standard heterosexual wedding almost pale in comparison. The sense of love and community was just astounding.

Over the years, we've been on a zillion protests. They're always kind of moving and whatnot. But protests are usually fueled by anger. This was prompted entirely by love and commitment. It was just amazing. And I don't know that I'll ever experience anything like it again in my life.

Flowers from the Heartland

Soon after City Hall opened its doors to lesbian and gay couples on February 12, media coverage flooded the nation with images of the pairs waiting in line and then emerging with marriage licenses. Americans living elsewhere in the country who wanted to participate in San Francisco's historic action quickly discovered the Internet as a means of inspiration. A movement developed through e-mail and blog messages that became known as "Flowers from the Heartland." People around America wanting to show support for the events in San Francisco donated money to buy flowers to be passed out freely to the same-sex partners married at City Hall. Notes would accompany the flowers, with messages such as, "To a happy couple, with love from Minneapolis."

Michael Ritz, the owner of Church Street Flowers in San Francisco, pointed out that over half of the four thousand married gay and lesbian couples received flowers in this way. He and his staff worked sixteen-hour days for almost the entire Month of Marriages. As a measure of the number of bouquets and boutonnieres distributed, Ritz said that his store's usual Valentine's Day retail sales were about $8,000, followed by days with sales in the range of $500 to $1,000. However, for the Winter of Love (the first weekend of which included Valentine's Day), Church Street Flowers took in an additional $15,000 of flowers *at cost* for the couples. Ritz indicated that these flowers' retail value would be between two and three times that amount. Moreover, Church Street Flowers was just one of many San Francisco florists participating in Flowers from the Heartland.

The economic impact of Mayor Newsom's decision to open up marriage to same-sex couples was substantial. Molly McKay of Marriage Equality California observed that, not only was the city awash with flowers, but "true to the history of our state, in this modern gold rush, the jewelers around town ran out of rings."

Supervisor Aaron Peskin also recognized the profitable effect.

We continued doing marriages on Monday of Presidents' Day/ Valentine's Day weekend, even though it was a city holiday. Early that morning, someone called me at home and said, "Put your suit on and come down here. There's a line still stretching around the block. We need help." Fine. So I came down here [to City Hall] and started doing weddings. I got my vows out, grabbed the next couple in line, talked to them for a minute, and married them up.

My wedding vows are in here somewhere [rummaging around in a desk drawer, then taking the vows out]. My handy-dandy wedding vows, right. You never know when you might need them. Here's where you put the certificate that they get from the Registrar that has personal information like where you're born and where you live.

So I said to these two guys, "Are you here on vacation?" "No, we flew out on the red-eye. We've been in line since six o'clock this morning." It was like two o'clock in the afternoon then. They were both from Florida. They'd read about it, got on an airplane, and out they came. The guy said to me, "Do you know a nice hotel to stay at?" "Yeah." "A place we can get rings?" "Oh, yeah." And so I'm thinking, sales tax, hotel tax. This is *good*!

They took their picture together and off they went. A few days later, I was running out of City Hall for a meeting in Chinatown, and a news reporter came up to me. There was a huge media circus going on for like a month. He stuck his camera in my face, and I said, "I can't. I'm late. I can't." "This'll just take thirty seconds." "Okay." "Supervisor, there's a Web site out of Florida saying that people should boycott San Francisco. What's your response?" And I replied, "I just married two gentlemen from Tampa." [He broke into hearty laughter.]

According to Assessor Mabel Teng's analysis, 91 percent of the 4,037 licenses were issued to couples living in California. Among the rest, only the states of Maine, Mississippi, West Virginia, and Wyoming were not represented, while seventeen couples came from Canada, Denmark, France, Germany, the Netherlands, Switzerland, Thailand, and the United Kingdom.

The Nullification

San Francisco's Chief Deputy City Attorney Therese Stewart and Deputy City Attorney Sherri Sokeland Kaiser mused about the California Supreme Court's voiding the same-sex marriages.

Stewart: Before issuing a decision, and in the decision itself, the court went out of its way to say that it wasn't deciding the underlying constitutional issues of whether marriage can be restricted to hetero-sexual couples, consistent with equal protection or due process. They said they were going to reserve that issue and let it come up through the trial courts and address it at a later time. They were looking solely at the issue of the mayor and city officials' authority to decide that a state statute is unconstitutional and then take action based upon that decision, before getting a judicial determination of the issue.

So I take them at their word that they're not prejudging the constitutional issue. I don't read much into the [August 2004] decision, other than that they had a very, very strong reaction to the idea that a local official would be able to make a constitutional decision and then act on it without first taking it to the courts and waiting for a decision there. I think the court felt preempted.

Kaiser: As an attorney working very diligently on this case, and being steeped in it, I was very clear about the argument we made. If Mayor Newsom was right, and if these statutes limiting marriage to a man and a woman are unconstitutional, then they're unconstitutional now, just as much as they would be after a court ruled. That was one of the strongest bases we had asking the court to wait in terms of making a decision about the marriages themselves.

But the court didn't, and I think it reached out to invalidate the marriages when there was good reason not to do so. To me, that felt like a particular slap, given the preciousness of the right and the length of time that it's been withheld and the need for our families to be protected in the same ways – the good arguments that the court could have turned to in order to defer deciding on the marriages.

We weren't asking them to validate the marriages. We were saying, regardless of what you think about what the mayor did, you can't quite decide whether the marriages are valid until you know if those statutes are constitutional.

Stewart: I think the court took our argument seriously. We got two dissents on the issue of leaving the licenses intact. But this is a middle-of-the-road court, in terms of their look at the world. They are neither far to the right nor far to the left politically. And they're not prone to extremes. I think uncertainty and hanging questions bother these particular individuals. It's just part of who they are. Much as I was upset about their not leaving the licenses intact, and felt that it was the wrong decision, I don't believe it was a kick in the teeth or intentionally designed to demean people. I really think it was about the mind-set of justices who just have trouble. ...

It could take a year or two for the constitutional issue to resolve itself. Having decided that they would wait for the lower courts to act, the justices weren't comfortable with the notion of just leaving the validity of these licenses up in the air and with the fact that that would create uncertainty for other people. We thought that those issues of uncertainty were far outweighed by the dignitary interests of the couples, at least in leaving the issue unresolved. But in the sense of their personal constitutions, these justices just had trouble with that.

Molly McKay of Equality California offered another perspective on the court's nullification.

What a weird thing it was, and how strangely it happened.

As soon as the antigay forces realized what was going on in San Francisco, they went to court for a restraining order. No one really anticipated that we would have a full month of marriages. The trial judges didn't see any immediate irreparable harm by continuing the marriages and refused to issue temporary restraining orders. The opposition then had to appeal to the California Supreme Court to stop what was happening.

The city of San Francisco, the state of California, and the antigay groups were involved in the litigation, but no one in the lawsuit represented the married couples. Our organization had tried to intervene and was denied the opportunity. We were at the courthouse on the day of oral argument. They refused to let us into the courtroom and put us in a side room instead. So we watched the debate live on a big movie screen. The antigay groups got not one, but two opportunities to speak to the court. It felt as though we had no voice, which was so disempowering and frustrating. We sat there seeing our lives debated and discussed, and there was no one, not even symbolically, representing the couples.

So that day was pretty awful, although it was heartening to hear some of the justices asking the larger, broader questions. But we knew it wasn't going to go our way. The decision made sense on the very narrow question that the court addressed. I don't have an objection to that. Nonetheless, over eight thousand people were impacted, plus all their children. It was an emotional setback, if nothing else.

Yet the experience taught me a valuable political lesson: be prepared for the worst-case scenario. We were ready for the supreme court to rule the way it did and had the opportunity to organize politically. We had talking points ready and had statewide meetings with our different community partners. So the moment the court ruled, we put into place a plan we'd set up.

We got in the streets and talked about how this impacted us. And not just in San Francisco, but all across the state. It was the largest statewide effort in support of gay rights that's ever happened. We had actions taken in twenty-five counties simultaneously. That was incredibly empowering. So we took a moment where it could have gone to the other side – technically, they won – and turned it around, by showing people crying who had been together up to forty years, and people holding their children and asking what this means to them. It was an opportunity to ask why this arbitrary, cruel decision was inflicted on these people, when all they wanted to do was protect their families. It was really a personal story we took to the issue. I think that changed it and moved us forward, almost more than the initial issuance of the licenses.

And it was on the front page of every single local paper. It even made the *New York Times*. You had Jennifer and Theresa on the front page of the *Ukiah Daily Journal* [in Mendocino County, 120 miles northwest of San Francisco]. Ladies in their late fifties who've been together forever, who live in everybody's backyard, and lots of people know them. Instead of "What's San Francisco doing in response to the court decision?" it was all of these different statewide activities. We had people in Placer County [140 miles northeast of San Francisco]. We had people in Fresno [180 miles southeast] and San Diego [500 miles southeast]. That presented something much more than just a single spokesperson responding on behalf of the gay rights movement. It was a community reacting.

So we found another opportunity to put a human face on the issue. We let people know, "This is our pain. This is why we're afraid. These are our families at stake. This isn't a political debate. It's our lives." That's what will change the issue. That's the political lesson I learned.

Future Court Action

San Francisco's lesbian and gay leadership is cautiously optimistic about what the California Supreme Court will do ultimately on the issue of whether the state's constitution requires recognition of same-sex marriage. Kate Kendell of the National Center for Lesbian Rights:

The court virtually invited an affirmative lawsuit [in March 2004] when it told the city to stop issuing marriage licenses. So I think the justices are more than prepared to hear the constitutional issue, and they'll be able to consider it in a context that isn't distorted by what Mayor Newsom did.

The supreme court sits here [in San Francisco]. Their offices are right across from City Hall. They have gay clerks. There are gay reporters who work for the legal newspapers, and the justices know that they're gay. This is a court that's familiar with gay men and lesbians. It's a very difficult – hopefully impossible – task to uphold a discriminatory classification of this type, not only based on the law and legal analysis, but also on knowing the people involved. This issue isn't an abstraction to these justices. It's not as though we're talking about, say, the Missouri Supreme Court. Rather, this is a court that's had regular interactions with gay people, and even colleagues who are gay, probably for most of the justices' lives. The heat that's behind the animosity toward gays elsewhere in the country is just gone here. This is the kind of hearts-and-minds contact that we're going to have to make nationwide, because when we can get courts to look at the law objectively, I think we'll always win.

San Francisco's Chief Deputy City Attorney Stewart and Deputy City Attorney Kaiser offered further reasons for lesbian and gay Californians to be hopeful about their state courts.

Stewart: This is the first case where the city itself has been a party to the litigation and has raised the issues on behalf of same-sex couples. There are clearly political aspects to that, because lots of lesbian and gay people live here.

In addition to that, the city studied the issue and found that the cost to the city of discriminating and not having couples married was more than $10 million a year. The state had a comparable study done, which showed the same thing ["The marginal effect [to California] of allowing same-sex couples to marry ... will be $28 million to $30 million per year, driven largely by the increased number of couples marrying, as well as the new impact on state income tax revenues" (Badgett and Sears 2005: 231)]. So did the federal government.

The key factor is that intact families – where you have two people responsible to each other for support, and for any children of that union – mean that every family member is less likely to end up dependent upon government benefits, whether welfare, Social Security, or medical care. Rather, intact families are more likely to have benefits through the workplace. They're more likely to have stable incomes. And because they have the legal obligations to each other that marriage creates, if one partner incurs expenses for medical or other benefits, the other marriage partner is obligated as well, and the government can collect on that if need be. So from an economic standpoint, it's just nuts for the government to not include them. That's a powerful economic reality, and this case brings that out in a way that no private case has done before.

Kaiser: Consider what's happening here in terms of what's happening elsewhere in the country, and frankly, around the world. Those countries that, like ours, embrace the ideals of equality and human dignity and are really willing to go out there in their jurisprudence and ensure that's what happens, those countries are uniformly adopting same-sex marriage rights. And that's what's going to happen in our country, too, because of our commitment to those values.

Other countries where it's already happened [Belgium, Canada, the Netherlands, and Spain] don't have as strong a conservative religious contingent, where the most vociferous opposition is coming from in this country. This issue has not been all that important for people in the middle. It's only just come up on their radar screens because of developments around the country. Those folks largely never thought about gays and lesbians getting married. When they think about it in the abstract, they say, "Umm. New. Different. We were taught, at least at some point, that gays and lesbians were bad. Ahhh, I don't know. Uncomfortable."

But San Francisco put a human face on the issue and showed people all the families that came to be married and the pent-up demand for it and the dignity of the process. That's really powerful, not just for that big group of people in the middle, but also for the judges making these decisions. Suddenly, it's not a hypothetical exercise. People now know there are a lot of us affected by this and for whom it's very important, and we're not a bunch of freaks. We're neighbors, we're friends. We look a lot like any other family.

So I think these two things – both our nation's commitment to equality in general, as a value that we really hold dear, and the greater humanity that is being attached to this issue – are really going to make it triumph sooner or later.

This optimism has been validated at the trial-court level. In March 2005, San Francisco Superior Court Judge Richard Kramer invalidated California's ban on same-sex marriage (*Coordination Proceeding*). Kate Kendell described the decision.

> Judge Kramer's ruling is fascinating, and so atypical of recent lower-court decisions from other states. He writes a twenty-some-page opinion, finding in unequivocal terms that not permitting lesbian and gay couples to marry is unconstitutional under the California Constitution. And he never uses the words "gay," "lesbian," "homosexual," or "sexual orientation." He never talks about the couples. He never discusses their stories or their lives or that they are human beings who deserve. ... Rather, he writes like a Republican would write this decision, which is what he is.
>
> He rules on gender discrimination, which in California gets strict judicial scrutiny, and the fundamental right to marry, which also gets strict scrutiny. He finds, as a matter of law, that this discrimination is unsupportable. He also says, even were strict scrutiny not to apply, there's no rational basis for upholding the discrimination. Just because there's a long tradition of discriminating doesn't make it right.
>
> Kramer is the sort of judge who *rarely* gets overturned on appeal, precisely because he writes the kinds of opinions that he wrote in this case. It's a decision that's unassailable from a legal standpoint, just looking at the law, taking out the issue of gay identity – which is absent from the ruling, and which I think is purposeful. The only way that this judgment could be overturned is if there's a panel on the Court of Appeal that doesn't like gay people. Because if they like the law, and they adhere to the rule of law, his decision is locked up tight.

Backlash

Five days after George W. Bush was selected for a second presidential term, the *New York Times* published an article (Belluck 2004) that began:

> In deconstructing the Democratic Party's Election Day failure, a number of fingers have been pointing to the push for same-sex marriage. ...

Senator Diane Feinstein, the California Democrat, said that the thousands of same-sex weddings at San Francisco City Hall "did energize a very conservative vote." She added: "So I think that whole issue has been too much, too fast, too soon. And people aren't ready for it." Other Democrats are privately saying similar things.

Whether the reemergence in 2003–2004 of same-sex marriage as a prominent political debate assured Republican Party dominance in the 2004 general election is seriously contested and addressed more systematically in the last chapter. Yet such overt criticism of over-whelmingly Democratic San Francisco by California's senior Democratic politician is itself a notable event, with Senator Feinstein directly disputing the political judgment of her successor (by several decades) as mayor, Gavin Newsom.

NCLR's Kate Kendell responded to the Feinstein challenge.

There's a reason they call it a civil rights *struggle*. If you told the truth to Power, and Power said, "Oh, you know, that's so true. You're *absolutely* right. *What* are we *doing* discriminating against you!? We're sorry. Here, enjoy your rights now," it wouldn't be a struggle. You wouldn't have past civil rights battles where people suffered much more and the tolls taken on their communities were far more severe than for us.

So I say, particularly to white queer folks, get over yourselves. This is what it means to be engaged in a fight for your dignity and humanity.

You will never have a moment in any civil rights struggle where all the forces arrayed against you say, "Okay, why don't you move forward now?" It's *never* the right time. What this demands is that people be engaged and take some risks on their own initiative in order to move issues forward in a difficult political environment.

I don't believe this political climate is going to change in two years or four. The fact of the matter is, we knew we were going to lose all of those state constitutional amendments [in 2004]. And many of them were already in process after Massachusetts, before Mayor Newsom did anything.

To satisfy the naysayers who complain that we're moving too quickly, you'd not only have to put a gag on the mayor and tell him not to do what he did, but you'd also have to roll back the Massachusetts decisions. Likewise with Vermont civil unions and the Hawaii court ruling.

At what point are we willing to say, "Oh, let's not make anybody mad by pushing for equality and fairness." I reject that. This is going to be a two-decade-long slog. And yes, it will be painful, and yes, some people will be hurt.

Gay folks in my home state of Utah are already suffering. Many people in other Red states are going to as well. We're not abandoning them. We're going back to those states to try and get whatever protections we can in this climate. But these aren't places that were going to promote marriage equality anytime soon anyway.

So I propose a dose of reality and a sense of history for folks who say, "Stop. You're making people mad." We have to stop doing that to ourselves.

Proposition 22 and a Future Same-Sex Marriage Ballot Measure

Despite California's history as a leader in recognizing relationship rights, the state legislature amended the Family Code in 1977 to limit marriage to a man and a woman. Then, in March 2000, some 61 percent of California voters approved Proposition 22, called the "Knight Initiative" after its author, Republican state senator Pete Knight. The ballot measure further amended the Family Code to read, "Only marriage between a man and a woman is valid and recognized in California." Its immediate effect was to ban recognition of same-sex marriages performed elsewhere.

The political campaign over Proposition 22 was hotly contested, and the measure's passage prompted the creation of a new lesbian and gay interest group, recounted by Molly McKay.

A lot of folks were disillusioned with the campaign that had been run against Proposition 22, the Knight Initiative. People were really disappointed with the "No on 22" campaign. Polls had shown that arguing that the initiative was discriminatory, divisive, and unnecessary resonated the most with nongay people. So part

95

of the campaign's strategy was not to reason in favor of same-sex relationship equality.

Many volunteers in the No-on-22 campaign staffed phone banks, only to be told by the people they called, "Listen, you homophobe, I'm not on your side. I'll never be with you. I support full equality." And, click, they'd hang up, despite our following a script that had been developed for us to a "T." So we lost both the battle and the war, by not moving the education forward through talking about the importance of our lives and relationships.

Out of the ashes of that campaign, then, arose Marriage Equality California, focused on doing the positive educational work about our lives and relationships that's eventually going to make this winnable in California. We've done a lot of visibility things around the issue. On Freedom to Marry Day, we go to county clerks' offices and ask for marriage licenses, knowing we'll be turned down. We do this statewide, get all dressed up and stand in line. We make friends with other people waiting there, talking about how long we've been together and sharing stories. They realize that we're very similarly situated, wanting to get married for many of the same reasons. We get to the front of the line, and the straight couple we've been talking with gets their marriage license without any questions asked and watch as we are turned down.

Our goal in doing this is to make visible the invisible discrimination that goes on every day at county clerks' offices. Usually they don't have to turn gay people down because they never see us. So to demonstrate the pain we experience from the legal discrimination, we go down and make a symbolic challenge to that rule.

Public opinion in California about same-sex marriage was mixed and in flux during 2004, as in much of the United States. Molly McKay described her perception of it in December of that year.

If you look at the polls, between 37 and 40 percent of Californians are ready for marriage equality for same-sex couples. Another third of the state's population thinks that gays and lesbians should have the same legal rights and protections afforded married couples, but want it called something different, like civil unions. So combining the two percentages produces 70 to 72 percent of the people in California ready for full legal equality for same-sex couples.

We see the education we need to do as explaining why civil unions are less than equal, both substantively and symbolically. We also have to make the distinction between civil marriage and religious marriage, and clarify religious freedoms issues. The domestic partnerships we have now in California are essentially civil unions. We have to show how they are still inadequate and extend only to the four corners of the state. Thus we know our job – doing the public education and the political work necessary to prepare communities and neutralize part of the opposition. Ultimately, we think this is a no-brainer when you get to the merits of the argument.

But there's a lot of misinformation put out by the other side. Combating disinformation in fact is the biggest hurdle to over-come. "Marriage between a man and woman – it's just that simple" is a very easy slogan. It's not quite as easy to explain to the disinterested middle that won't give much time to the matter that, actually, same-sex couples are living in the same situations as their opposite-sex counterparts.

This stupid, horrible new trend of constitutional amendments means that this is going to be hand-to-hand combat, where we have to win by a popular vote of the people in a state with 16 million registered voters.

If we lose, it won't matter for the California Supreme Court to apply the equal protection clause to marriage discrimination and hold it unconstitutional. That's very frustrating. But the public education system apparently hasn't worked effectively, because people don't get their civics. They no longer know that there are three branches of government, and each has an important role. The judiciary is a check and balance on the tyranny of the majority. That's now out the window. It's not fair. It's not right. But it's the reality. We're dealing with it, and we're moving for-ward with it, because we have no other choice.

Kate Kendell hoped for legislative action endorsing same-sex marriage before a popular vote on amending the state constitution.

Once same-sex marriages are a reality, the alleged dangers of gay
people getting married can be disproved. You can't rebut the
falsehoods that are being spun by the folks arrayed in the antigay
movement until gay people are married. The best antidote to the
fear of nervous and concerned people is gay people getting married – and then their wives not leaving them, and heterosexual
people still wanting to get married. In other words, the parade of
horribles doesn't happen.

In September 2005, Kendell's wish for legislatively sanctioned
marriage for lesbian and gay couples moved close to fruition. That
month, as a result of tenacious effort by Mark Leno, San Francisco's
gay assemblyman, the California State Senate, by a vote of 21 to 15,
and then the assembly, by a 41-to-35 vote, approved a bill to legalize
same-sex nuptials. However, Governor Arnold Schwarzenegger
vetoed the measure, invoking Proposition 22 and stating: "[T]he
matter should be determined not by legislative action – which would
be unconstitutional – but by court decision or another vote of the
people of our state. We cannot have a system where the people vote
and the Legislature derails that vote" (Murphy 2005). Nonetheless,
California's action was the first by an American legislature to
authorize same-sex marriage.

Unlike Massachusetts, where the General Court must be involved
in the constitutional amendment process, California permits citizen
initiatives without legislative participation. If proposed changes to
the Golden State's charter receive the designated number of voter
signatures on petitions, then the measures go directly to the people
at the next election. Accordingly, interest groups may bypass the
legislature in their attempts to make state policy.

With this procedural attribute in mind, two conservative groups –
ProtectMarriage.com and VoteYesMarriage.com – competed in
2005 for a citizen initiative to add a same-sex marriage ban to the
California Constitution. The two amendments differed on whether
to rescind the legislatively enacted domestic partnership benefits for
same-sex couples. Polling by ProtectMarriage.com indicated that
a majority of California voters supported a same-sex marriage

prohibition but not a repeal of the domestic partner rights. Accordingly, the goal of the ProtectMarriage.com constitutional amendment was more modest than that of VoteYesMarriage.com.

After a five-month volunteer effort that concluded at the end of 2005, a signature drive by ProtectMarriage.com came up about 200,000 signatures short of the 598,000 needed on petitions to qualify for the ballot. At the same time, VoteYesMarriage.com postponed its petition campaign in order to raise money to hire professional signature gatherers ("Group Drops Bid to Ban Same-Sex Marriage" 2005). Thus, a California referendum on same-sex marriage appears unlikely for 2006.

Yet LGBT interest groups are planning for an eventual popular vote on gay marraige in the Golden State, especially in the event that the California Supreme Court strikes down the statutory ban on same-sex nuptials. Molly McKay of Marriage Equality California elaborated on her organization's efforts to respond to a ballot initiative.

> We've been doing the groundwork and have a campaign ready to go. We've learned lessons from other states that have had these battles. This is a person-by-person struggle. It's a neighbor-to-neighbor, family-member-to-family-member, coworker-to-coworker challenge to get our message across. It's not a difficult conversation to have, and it's pretty easy to get people educated on the subject. But you have to take the time to do it. So it's a pretty daunting campaign in a state as large as California.
>
> First of all, we have a structure of between one and four chapter leaders in each county, depending on size. They are in charge of having monthly meetings and public events and getting in contact with elected officials. They are the catchall persons in their communities to talk about marriage and to ensure that marriage *is* being talked about. Also, these are the best people to tell us how to communicate effectively about marriage in their communities. How you discuss marriage equality is going to be different in Fresno than in Berkeley or San Diego.
>
> The other lesson we've learned is that who the messenger is is just as important as the message itself. So we're building alliances with religious coalition leaders to go out into religious

communities to have the conversations, because there are dialogues where we don't always have the language and standing necessary to communicate effectively.

We also hope to co-found an Asian-Pacific-Islander coalition of organizations for marriage equality. We've linked up speakers statewide and supported rallies in California's API community. There's a similar effort with the National Black Justice Coalition. A number of its members here in California are doing great work. We also hope to co-found a "Latinos for Marriage Equality" group. So there will be many communities engaged in dialogue about same-sex marriage around the state.

Our plan and strategy represent a web. Each strand is delicate, and they go in all different directions. But if you put enough strands together, they become one of the strongest materials known to science.

So that's what we're doing. We're a small organization, with only six staff people statewide. So it's a Herculean volunteer effort, with a huge coalition of partners throughout California.

San Francisco Chief Deputy City Attorney Stewart critiqued the prospect of popular votes on same-sex marriage.

The extreme, vociferous, fundamentalist Christian minority in the country has been very loud for a long time on gay rights. Our issues are politically useful for the right, because they take the focus off things like the war in Iraq and other much more pressing matters. Indeed, the religious right needs somebody to hate. There's always a scapegoat that God is condemning in their view. There has to be a villain of the day for them.

Then there's this big swath of middle America, which hasn't really thought very deeply about the issue. It hasn't been high on their radar screen. They're just beginning to get used to gay men and lesbians being out and living in their communities, as opposed to being found just in urban areas where, not only are gays fully out and participating, but also pushing for rights more strongly than in the middle of the country.

These Americans aren't people of the world, and for a long time, they've heard the message that filters through some of the churches about our having a different "lifestyle" than straight people. And that lifestyle's all about sex. You know, heterosexuality is not about sex, but somehow homosexuality is. They've been told that we won't be good citizens and that we'll convert everybody else to being gay, which is assumed to be bad. So all these bugaboos persist about society falling apart because of gay people.

The one fear you hear a lot is that we're out to destroy marriage as an institution. If gay people marry, it's going to take the meaning out of marriage. That has to be based upon an assumption that we're not really concerned about long-term, monogamous, committed relationships. But the only reason that gay people want their relationships to be sanctified in the way that marriage does is because we believe in them. People, whether straight or gay, who don't want to have that kind of relationship don't seek to get married.

FIVE

Oregon

Was there any domination which did not appear natural to those that possessed it?

– John Stuart Mill (quoted in Gerstmann 2005: 217)

THIRTEEN STATES PLACED state constitutional amendments limiting marriage to a union between a man and a woman on their ballots in 2004, and all passed by substantial margins. In addition to banning marriage for same-sex couples, amendments in nine of the thirteen states barred civil unions and domestic partnership arrangements for lesbian and gay pairs. Only 1996 had more state governmental action affecting gay men and lesbians, when fourteen states passed defense-of-marriage acts (Andersen 2005: 181). Table 5.1 summarizes the 2004 information.

Table 5.1. 2004 *Ballot initiatives and referenda banning same-sex marriage*

State	Yes–no vote (%)	Included civil unions?
Arkansas	75–25	Yes
Georgia	76–24	Yes
Kentucky	75–25	Yes
Louisiana	78–22	Yes
Michigan	59–41	Yes
Mississippi	86–14	No
Missouri	71–29	No
Montana	66–34	No
North Dakota	73–27	Yes
Ohio	62–38	Yes
Oklahoma	76–24	Yes
Oregon	57–43	No
Utah	66–34	Yes

The data reveal that the smallest margin of victory was in Oregon. Moreover, that state's amendment was one of only four not prohibiting civil unions and domestic partnerships. Among states adopting defense-of-marriage amendments in 2004, then, Oregon's action was the least antagonistic to gay people.

Oregon is further distinguished amid the states passing gay-marriage bans in 2004, because marriage licenses were actually issued to same-sex partners there. In March and April 2004, Multnomah County (containing Oregon's largest city, Portland), at the direction of its five-member county commission, gave marriage licenses to some three thousand lesbian and gay couples. This chapter tells the story of the only state in the nation (as of 2005) where same-sex pairs wed under color of law and where citizens then had the opportunity to vote on the legitimacy of that action.

Prologue

Oregon is like California in that interest groups may trigger policy making without legislative involvement. With five statewide initiatives and more than twenty-five local ones occurring between 1988 and 2004, the Beaver State has had more ballot measures directed at gay and lesbian rights than any other state in the nation (Andersen 2005: 144–145). Most were sponsored by the Oregon Citizens Alliance (OCA) under the leadership of Lon Mabon (Reed 1999). The first statewide initiative, Measure 8 of 1988, sought to repeal a governor's executive order prohibiting sexual-orientation discrimination in public employment. The measure passed with 53 percent of the vote, but was later struck down by the Oregon Court of Appeals as an unconstitutional infringement of free speech (*Merrick v. Board of Higher Education* 1992).

With Measure 9 in 1992, the OCA tried a more proactive approach to outlaw state and local laws prohibiting sexual-orientation discrimination.

All governments in Oregon may not use their monies or properties to promote, encourage or facilitate homosexuality, pedophilia, sadism, or masochism. All levels of government, including public educational systems, must assist in setting a standard for Oregon's youth which recognizes that these "behaviors" are "abnormal, wrong, unnatural, and perverse," and that they are to be discouraged and avoided. The State may not recognize this conduct under sexual orientation or sexual preference levels, or through quotas, minority status, affirmative action or similar concepts.

Measure 9 was defeated with 56 percent of the vote.

The OCA promoted its antigay agenda again in 1994, with Measure 13.

> Governments cannot: Create classifications based on homosexuality; Advise or teach children, students, or employees that homosexuality equates legally or socially with race or other protected classifications; Spend public funds in a manner promoting or expressing approval of homosexuality; Grant spousal benefits or marital status based on homosexuality; Deny constitutional rights or services due under existing statutes. Measure nonetheless allows adult library books addressing homosexuality with adult-only access. Public employees' private lawful sexual behaviors may be cause for personnel action, if those behaviors disrupt the workplace.

Measure 13 lost with 52 percent of the vote opposing it.

The last statewide initiative by the OCA was Measure 9 in 2000, which sought to prohibit public school instruction "encouraging, promoting, or sanctioning homosexual or bisexual behaviors." It was defeated with 53 percent of the vote.

This extensive history of ballot initiatives of importance to Oregon's lesbian and gay community forged one of the most politically sophisticated state gay rights organizations in the nation, Basic Rights Oregon (BRO). As well, Beaver State voters have had as much experience dealing with the politics of gay rights as any other Americans. Accordingly, Oregon's struggle for same-sex marriage offers a microcosm of the national debate concerning access by gay men and lesbians to civil marriage.

Multnomah County

Roey Thorpe, the executive director of Basic Rights Oregon, explained the circumstances leading up to the decision in March 2004 by the Multnomah County Commission to grant marriage licenses to same-sex couples.

BRO has a legal advisory group that was formed in 1999 or 2000. That group came together specifically on the issue of same-sex marriage. It was kind of ahead of its time. It was a group of attorneys who were working with Basic Rights Oregon and the ACLU, and they did some research and determined that then was not the right time. So they continued to meet regularly and help out BRO on a number of different projects, waiting until the time was right.

When the legal decisions started to happen [in 2003], this group immediately recognized the significance for their original intent. So for us, this started in the summer of 2003, after the [U.S. Supreme Court's] *Lawrence* decision. I remember the day after the decision, the press called me and asked, "Is gay marriage next?" And I said, "Oh, that's just what [Supreme Court] Justice [Antonin] Scalia is saying. That's a smokescreen. That's blah, blah, blah." Then the reporter said to me, "No, actually that's what gay rights activists are saying on the national level," and read me a couple of quotes. And I said, "Oh!" So a lot of people were thinking it was the next logical step.

Then, when the *Goodridge* decision happened, we immediately had some planning sessions where we went through and tried to figure out the best way to attain marriage equality in Oregon. We had a group of attorneys and a couple of political strategists, and we mapped out all the different options and did the pros and cons.

We eventually decided that the best way was to have couples get married. For a whole variety of reasons, getting couples married would be our best shot. We figured that there was a backlash coming anyway. Certainly, the [2004] State of the Union address only confirmed that belief. We knew that no matter what we did, Oregon was not a state that had a defense of marriage act at the time. So we knew that it was coming, no matter what. We thought, well, it might be helpful to have couples already married, and we would have gay people talking about what that meant to them.

We did some research and decided that the Multnomah County Commission was our best bet, although we had other options if they said no. Our planning was so detailed that we decided not to talk to them in December, because I wanted them to keep this quiet while they were doing the research. We didn't want someone to go to court and file an injunction before there were any marriages. So I decided not to approach the commissioners before Christmas, because I thought, if they said yes, it would be too hard for these wonderful commissioners, who had all these gay friends, to not tell their friends at Christmas parties. I just didn't think they'd be able to do it – not because they aren't incredibly professional and discrete, but because they would know how momentous and important it would be to their friends and family members.

When our group did its planning, and we talked about how getting couples married would be best, the first thing I did was to consult with the national gay and lesbian legal organizations. So I called Evan Wolfson [of Freedom to Marry]. I called Lambda [Legal Defense and Education Fund]. I called Kate Kendell [of the National Center for Lesbian Rights]. The ACLU. I described in detail what our plan was, and then we scheduled a conference call. We made our plan here [in Oregon], but we were very aware that this was a national movement. We didn't want to do anything that would in any way impede that movement or screw things up. And we were very interested in the input from the national organizations about where they saw Oregon in the mix and how Oregon compared to other states.

Everyone was very supportive, which surprised me. Because I think it's kind of rare that nobody says, "Oh, no, no, no. We have another plan." People were saying, "Yes. That makes sense." We were able to answer every question they had. So they gave us the go-ahead and their blessing and offered to be a resource to us.

In early January, our lobbyist, Maura Roche, and I went to the Multnomah County commissioners and asked them to issue marriage licenses to same-sex couples. We met with four of the five commissioners, two of them together, and then two individual meetings. We said to them that we believed, because of the legal decisions that had been made in the past year and the similarity of Oregon's Constitution to that of Massachusetts, that a strong argument could be made that it was illegal to deny same-sex partners these licenses. We asked them to go to their own legal counsel and ask that question. That is what started the ball rolling here.

The way this played out in the media was that San Francisco started issuing marriage licenses [in February 2004], and then it started popping up in other places. But in reality this was something that we were working with the commissioners on in January. The day that the marriages began in San Francisco, we actually were on a conference call with Kate Kendell, Evan Wolfson, and some folks from the ACLU and Lambda Legal, with our legal advisory group. We were talking about what was happening in Oregon as all that was starting in San Francisco. We really believed that we would be the first place in the country to do this.

[During the initial planning] we were thinking that our marriages would happen in May, June, maybe even later. And we had a few people from the [Portland] community calling us and saying, "Hey, are you guys going to push for same-sex marriage?"

Well, when San Francisco started marrying couples, it was like a floodgate. People were calling us up and saying, "What the hell are you doing?! Come on! We're going down and demanding marriage licenses." There was so much pressure on us. What people didn't know here was that things were already under way. That created a very tense situation.

I believe that, even if we hadn't done everything that we did, couples would have still gone down to the county, and they would have demanded marriage licenses. There were so many forces from so many different angles that it felt like we were both moving things forward and caught almost in this stampede. It was like the running of the bulls. I felt like, every time I looked around, there was something else happening, or moving forward, or pushing us. And it was just a really remarkable feeling.

At the same time as Basic Rights Oregon was responding to national legal and political events surrounding the topic of same-sex marriage, other people and organizations in the Beaver State were making plans as well. Tim Nashif, a founder and director of the Oregon Family Council, elaborated.

We understood Oregon's place in the battle that was going on nationally. Massachusetts was on the verge of legalizing same-sex marriage, not through the people but through the courts. So the question came up, if Massachusetts legalizes same-sex marriage, how do we deal with the fact that [gay and lesbian] Oregonians may be able to go to Massachusetts, get married, come back to Oregon, and then we have a situation in Oregon where there's this debate about whether these marriages should be recognized.

So we were struggling with that along with a lot of states that didn't necessarily have a clear law taking the matter into consideration. Our law in Oregon recognized marriage as between one man and one woman. [Oregon Revised Statutes, Chapter 506 reads: "Marriage is a civil contract entered into in person by males at least 17 years of age and females at least 17 years of age, who are otherwise capable, and solemnized in accordance with [another statutory section]." Such other section states that "the parties thereto shall assent or declare . . . that they take each other to be husband and wife."] But that [statute] didn't necessarily apply to marriages from out of state, number one, depending on how a court wanted to rule. And it certainly did not apply to any constitutional interpretation of Article 1, Section 20, of the Oregon Constitution. ["No law shall be passed granting to any citizen or class of citizens privileges, or immunities, which, upon the same terms, shall not equally belong to all citizens."] Based on all of that, the Oregon Family Council and a number of key pastors were trying to decide in late February [2004] what our best response would be.

At that time, our last choice would've been a ballot initiative dealing with the situation. Our first choice would have been, hey, maybe the feds will take care of the problem for us, through the Federal Marriage Amendment. So maybe what we should do is get in behind and support that. Because it's obvious that a lot of states other than Oregon have the problem.

The second option was through the Oregon Legislature. It's obviously a lot easier to deal with something like this through the legislature. When we spoke with the Oregon Legislature about it, they said, Hey look, we probably should deal with it, because it is going to be an issue. So that door was open. That was choice number two.

Choice number three was to do an initiative. There were a couple of reasons it was the third choice. First, we were running out of time. There really wasn't enough time left to seriously consider doing an initiative. In Oregon, there is a four-step appeal process, once you get your language in, for getting an initiative on the ballot. And there's no limit on the [Oregon] Supreme Court in that appeal process. They can spend sixty days or six months looking at the language of your ballot title, and it has never been done in less than sixty days. Once you do get your ballot title, and once you go through all the appeals, then you've got to gather a minimum of 130,000 signatures in order to have the hundred thousand that you need. So people doing initiatives in Oregon usually start two years before the general election of interest.

Here we are at the end of February and we're thinking we're not going to get our language until sometime in the middle of May, if we're lucky. That gives us about six to eight weeks [until July 2] to gather 130,000 signatures, which no one has ever done before. In fact, most of the signature drives for constitutional amendments fall short. Very, very few of them ever collect enough signatures for a constitutional amendment. They try, and spend lots of money, and never make it.

So that's what we were faced with. Plus initiatives are very expensive. You have to pay to gather, and figure out how to gather, the signatures. However you do it, whether through volunteers or paid collectors, a statewide campaign is very expensive. The Oregon Family Council had never done a ballot measure before on gay rights. We had been involved in other initiatives where we played a supporting role, but not the principal one.

Frankly, the general feeling on our board is that we don't like initiatives. We feel like the legislature is a good place to go. Those people are elected officials and ought to do their jobs. If we have a problem, they ought to be the ones to solve it. We believe the initiative process is necessary for those things where you can't reach agreement in the legislature. So there are occasions where the people ought to have their voice and need to be heard. We would not agree with everything being driven by an initiative process. That's very bad government.

So that's where we were at the end of February. Jeff Mapes, the chief political writer for the *Oregonian* [the leading Portland newspaper], met with me and four key Oregon pastors to get our feelings about same-sex marriage and what we felt was coming up and what the problems were. The three directions I just discussed were mentioned as options for us, but all in the context of Massachusetts. It was never in the context of Oregon because, number one, no one had ever tried to promote same-sex marriage in Oregon before. Number two, we have an Oregon law on the books that clearly states marriage is between one man and one woman. So it would have to become a judicial activist situation, which was a concern for us because of what happened in Massachusetts. No one had even thought of that as a big enough concern until what took place in Massachusetts.

We were convinced at that time to get behind a federal amendment, which we knew takes a long time, or to get our legislature to visit it. We thought we had time to come back later with an initiative if the legislature couldn't figure it out. We thought we had until 2006. We had four different versions [of ballot measures] that we submitted the language for towards the end of February, just in case the third option ended up being our only option. But we weren't real serious about it then.

Our language ["It is the policy of Oregon, and its political subdivisions, that only a marriage between one man and one woman shall be valid or legally recognized as a marriage"] lined up with the U.S. Constitution, in that it would cover any [same-sex] marriage that might come in from out-of-state. Because remember, when we drafted the language, we were thinking Massachusetts. That's where the words "it's the policy of Oregon" came from, because the U.S. Constitution refers to the policy of a particular state needing to be respected. And because we were concerned about a situation like San Francisco, where the mayor did it on his own – at the time, we didn't know Multnomah County was going to do it – we added the language, "and its political subdivisions" – technical language for any city, county, or other municipality.

In Oregon, we have a supreme court that has thrown out constitutional amendment initiatives after they passed because of what they call an Armada rule, which is a two-subject rule. They're saying a constitutional amendment cannot cover two subjects or more. So if we had also covered civil unions, for example, like other states did, that would perhaps be considered two subjects. We don't agree with the Armada. It's like judicial activism in a lot of ways. The people voted for it. It was clear what they wanted. And it was thrown out. So we were very concerned about that and wanted to make sure we kept it single subject. That was key.

On the afternoon of March 2, I had messages on my cell phone saying that [the Multnomah County decision to extend marriage licenses to same-sex couples] was going to come down first thing in the morning. The news had broken that afternoon about three or four o'clock. That was a Tuesday. At nine o'clock that Wednesday morning, the county commissioners had a press conference and announced that the Constitution of Oregon demanded that they give out marriage licenses [to same-sex couples], and in one hour, they were going to start giving out marriage licenses.

We found out later that they had been working diligently with Roey [Thorpe] and Basic Rights Oregon for several months behind the scenes to put this together. In fact, not only did they have people at ten o'clock lining up around the corner to get marriage licenses, they'd also rented a large facility for massive ceremonies. Apparently, they felt that they could get shut down in twenty-four hours, that a lawsuit could be filed and be pushed to the [Oregon] Supreme Court. They were making sure that some [gay and lesbian] people got licenses and got married.

So I think they realized that whatever they were doing might not hold for very long, that they needed to do it very quickly and quietly, even to the point of leaving one commissioner, Lonnie Roberts, totally out of the process. He would clearly not have been in agreement. So all of the commissioner meetings were without him. The press was left out of the process. The public was left out of the process. The only ones brought into the process were the four county commissioner women who were in favor of it and Basic Rights Oregon, their activist entourage and their attorneys. They worked out all the details of this subversive – in our minds – activity.

I was very discouraged to hear [what the Multnomah County Commission had done]. I was having a difficult time believing it because there was no due process. There were no hearings. There were no open meetings. This state is independent-minded. People do like to know what's going on and be included in the process. In Oregon, you hardly cut a tree down without a public meeting. So to make a policy decision like this behind closed doors . . . . We even have very clear public meeting laws on our books, that if policy changes are going to be made . . . . And here we have a statute in Oregon that clearly defines marriage as between one man and one woman. These commissioners decided on their own accord to disregard a statute.

A statute on the books in Oregon doesn't get there easily. It gets there because the legislature votes for it after many committee hearings, and then it goes to the governor for signature. So it's not like they violated some little resolution. They violated an Oregon statute to do this because they felt that the statute was unconstitutional and it was their right and responsibility to make that ruling.

[The Multnomah County commissioners] could've done a variety of other things if they felt that there was a constitutional breach by a law that had been on the books for 142 years. What they should've done is have a conversation with the executive branch and say, Hey look, we think this violates the Oregon Constitution. At that point, the Attorney General either agrees or disagrees. If they agree, then they write an opinion and send it to the legislature and say [ORS] 106 could be unconstitutional. Or go to the courts and ask for a ruling on this. That could very easily have been done before the fact.

The commissioners have authority in Multnomah County, but it's not their job to make decisions for the state of Oregon. They took the law into their own hands. To them, it was a strategy. To us, it was bad public policy, and a horrible direction to take people down. People were irritated and terribly alarmed by it. Even those who might have been in favor of same-sex marriage didn't like the way this came down.

We felt that [the commissioners and Basic Rights Oregon] had declared war on the people of Oregon. We normally would call something like this a difference of opinion. But we can hardly look at it as a difference of opinion because of the way they went about it. Oregonians who didn't agree with it had no choice in voicing their opinion on the subject matter in advance. As statewide politics go, four minor-player women in one county made a decision for all Oregonians without any public meetings and in secret. The only organization they brought into the process was Basic Rights Oregon. And they relied on them to pull all the pieces together. Based on that, we looked at it as a declaration of war on the people of Oregon, more so than as a difference of opinion.

Kelly Clark, a former Republican member of the Oregon Legislature and the attorney who represented the sponsors of Measure 36, the 2004 initiative banning same-sex marriage, elaborated on the objection to the Multnomah County action.

The case for gay marriage is a case for a new constitutional right. But unlike the question of race, for example, we have never had a constitutional dialogue on gay rights at all. And unlike questions of gender, age, or other traits, we have never even had a legislative or public debate on gay rights in the context of marriage.

Process and substance are one and the same when it comes to constitutional dialogue. You can't separate them out and say, "Well, we were right on the merits. So even though we broke all the rules, we should get what we're asking for." No, no, no, no, no. Process and substance are one and the same.

Once you have a constitutional consensus, you have every right in the world to seek redress in the courts. Because then you're asking the courts to do what they're supposed to do, which is enforce constitutional rights. You're not putting them in that difficult place where they're really being asked to be arbiters of social justice without guidance from the population.

I'm actually more of a constitutional judicial conservative than a political conservative. It makes guys like me very, very nervous when the ACLU shows up in the courtroom and says, "Declare it to be unconstitutional and grant same-sex marriage," and they can't point to any place in the state constitution or statutes where there's even a hint of guidance from the people. It just strikes me as getting the cart before the horse.

I grew up in Little Rock, Arkansas, and remember having to leave my home in the 1950s because of concerns about riots. There was a whole group of people in the middle, not the hard-core racists and not the do-gooder integrationists. But a whole group of people in the middle were kind of watching all of this with great interest. Once federal troops got called in, and [segregationist Governor] Orville Faubus got stared down, there was a whole group of people in the middle that said, "Well, of course, that's the way it should have gone anyway."

Because the rule of law matters. People follow the rule of law. There's at least a significant portion of people in the middle that will follow the rule of law, even when they disagree with it. For that reason, a constitutional consensus is important, because the guys who won can say, "We won fair and square. And this is the rule of law now." It's like winning a football game on a bad call. You still won. The game is over. You've advanced to the next round of the playoffs. If people want to gripe about the bad call, they can gripe about it. That's how, that's why a consensus matters.

The Defense of Marriage Coalition

Tim Nashif described the formation of the Oregon Defense of Marriage Coalition, which sponsored Measure 36.

The night before [Multnomah County] started giving out the licenses, a group of us got together in a conference call. We made a decision that we were going to have to look at all of our options now. So we had to push our initiative and at least give it a try. Because if you play it out, and the legislature doesn't deal with it, and the courts don't deal with it, then we're at where Massachusetts is. We're giving out marriage licenses for two or three years before we have the initiative to deal with it.

On Wednesday, March 3, at nine o'clock in the morning, they had their press conference and started issuing licenses at ten o'clock. We met at the county commissioners' headquarters at two o'clock in the afternoon and had our press conference. Kelly Clark was there. I had three or four key pastors, representing the largest churches in the state, with four, five, six, seven thousand church members. I had two state legislators there. I had the county commissioner there who was boxed out of the process. And we announced the beginning of the Defense of Marriage Coalition. Representatives from the African-American community were there and spoke.

We said we're going to the legislature, and even though we don't think we have time, we're trying like heck to get an initiative on the ballot. And the big questions from the press were, "Gee, don't you think it's too late?" "How long do you think you need to gather signatures?" I thought the best that we could hope for was, if we had eight weeks, we might get it done. But nobody had ever done it before.

We spoke to the Speaker of the House. The senate was split,
15-15 [between Democrats and Republicans]. At that time, they
hadn't even elected a president yet. There was no real leader there.
The Speaker of the House agreed with us that, in a special session,
she would bring the issue up and deal with it. She agreed that if we
did not get our initiative, she would deal with it. Bear in mind that
legislators were not reacting to us. They were ticked on their
own. We didn't have to help them. Everybody was grieved by
the way this came down. Basically, it was very easy for us [in the
legislature].

The first thing the Defense of Marriage Coalition did after its
news conference was seek judicial intervention, as explained by
Kelly Clark.

We filed the initial court challenge within three days of the
Multnomah County decision to start issuing same-sex licenses. It
was a straightforward claim that they violated the public meetings
law, which says that we have open meetings and advance notice of
things. We [also] asked for a declaration that the state [marriage]
statute was not unconstitutional.

We went to court and sought a temporary restraining order
[TRO] to stop [Multnomah County] from issuing any more
licenses. Multnomah County filed papers to dismiss our case,
saying that none of my clients had standing. The ACLU, representing Basic Rights Oregon, and a number of gay couples
filed motions to intervene in the case. We did not oppose the
intervention.

So we had a TRO hearing in early March, and we lost. The
judge did not rule on the standing question. He decided he did not
have to reach that issue, because we had not shown irreparable
harm. His reasoning was, once the initial licenses were issued,
there was no additional harm in continuing to issue licenses. So
whether there were thirty licenses issued, or three thousand, we
couldn't prove irreparable harm.

As we were regrouping and trying to figure out where to go from
there, the governor and the Attorney General's office began to
weigh in. I forget the exact sequence of events, but at some point
Benton County – down in Corvallis, home of Oregon State University – started making noises about issuing same-sex marriage

licenses. Then there were rumblings in Lane County – in Eugene, where the University of Oregon is located. At that point, the governor got pretty heavily involved, working behind the scenes to keep these counties backed off while we tried to get a political solution worked out. The governor is a former attorney general and state supreme court justice. He has a statewide perspective and didn't like a piecemeal, county-by-county approach to this.

Fairly quickly after that, the idea came up that Basic Rights Oregon and the ACLU would file a lawsuit against Multnomah County and the state over the registration of the existing licenses, and that my clients would be permitted to intervene. That case would be put on a fast track through the trial court and appellate courts. So we bought off on that, because there was still the standing challenge for the initial lawsuit. Standing for intervention is a much less severe hurdle.

My perception – and I argued this both to the ACLU and the state – was that they needed us to be involved in the case. By this point, the Attorney General had concluded that, in his opinion, the marriage statute was unconstitutional. My argument to them for why they should not oppose our intervention was, "If we're not in the game, then this case has no legitimacy as a political matter – because there would be nobody fighting to preserve the traditional institution of marriage in the case. And you need *us* in this case, as opposed to guys from the East Coast or the South," who were just chomping at the bit to get into this case. Some of the interest groups around the country wanted to take it and run with it.

So we sort of came to a procedural truce. The idea was, everybody would take part, and we'd put it on a fast track. We dismissed our original lawsuit without prejudice and decided to narrow the issues on the newly filed ACLU lawsuit.

In the ACLU lawsuit, [the trial judge's] ruling came down in the middle of April. On cross motions for summary judgment, after a very colorful series of hearings, he sort of split the baby, a Vermont-style approach. He said, to the extent that the Oregon marriage statutes deny the benefits of marriage to same-sex couples, then they violate our equal privileges and immunities clause of Article 1, Section 20 [of the Oregon Constitution].

However, he ruled that the definitional statute – marriage between one man and woman – was not necessarily unconstitutional.

He would give the Oregon Legislature ninety days from the next legislative session to come up with a remedy for the privileges and immunities violation and benefits. If they didn't, then he would order Multnomah County to begin issuing same-sex marriage licenses. Basically, [it was] the same kind of "or else" that came out of Vermont: "You either remedy this problem on the benefits front, or I'll have to."

We had argued very, very aggressively that he should not order the legislature to do anything and that he should not issue a remedy. If he found a constitutional violation, he should stop there and defer to the legislature to try and craft whatever remedies they thought appropriate. The crux of our argument was that these plaintiffs were asking for something unprecedented. Without any constitutional text or history or statutory provision or ballot measure or administrative regulation or public hearings or anything, they were asking for the courts to create a new constitutional right.

The only surprising part of the whole [trial court] ruling was not even on the table for decision. The judge ordered the State Registrar to register the marriage licenses. Nobody quite knew what that meant. Was he saying that they were valid? Was it just an administrative function? Or what? He never really said.

Interestingly, [if you] fast-forward, after Measure 36 passed, it's the only remaining live question on appeal – what's the status of the three thousand marriage licenses? Are they valid? Not valid? Were they ever valid? Our position of course was that they were void *ab initio* [i.e., from the beginning] because the county clerk didn't have the authority to contravene the state statute.

The case went directly to the [Oregon] Court of Appeals, again on a fast track. The court of appeals turned around and certified it directly to the [Oregon] Supreme Court, taking itself out of the case, partly in response to the governor's request to get an early ruling. Then the supreme court accepted review on an expedited basis, [setting] oral argument for November.

When [Measure 36] passed, the supreme court pulled the oral argument date, asked for a new round of briefing as to what was left of the case in light of Measure 36, and set the argument for December 15. The plaintiffs in their [new] briefing said, Okay, now that marriage is off the table, civil unions should be the remedy. Well, they had argued against civil unions all throughout the case. They had said civil unions were separate but unequal and unconstitutional and all that. Then very quickly after Measure 36 passed, they changed their tactic and said, now you should consider this a case asking for civil unions and the benefits of marriage.

We screamed at that, saying, you can't change your lawsuit four-fifths of the way through, in front of the supreme court. They've got to go back and start over again with a new case. Nothing in Measure 36 says that they couldn't sue for civil unions or for benefits. But that wasn't what the case was all about from the beginning. It was a challenge to the marriage statutes.

I think the [supreme] court was troubled by the procedural mess that the case had become. The most interesting thing left was the sort of San Francisco question – does the local clerk have the authority to take matters into his own hands and issue marriage licenses, which are pretty clearly in contravention of state statute, if the clerk believes the state statutes are unconstitutional? That's the question I would expect we'd get some guidance on from the court, because there are some practical implications for the three thousand couples holding those licenses.

Measure 36

While Kelly Clark led the judicial charge on behalf of the Defense of Marriage Coalition, Tim Nashif focused on the ballot initiative.

When initiatives are submitted to the [Oregon] Secretary of State, the AG [Attorney General] looks at the language. They have so many days to do that, and as is their custom, they don't give you your language until five o'clock on the last day allowed. They never do it early. Then people have time to look at the language, and those on the other side have a chance to submit their reasons why the language is crummy.

We looked at the AG's language and said we had no problem with it. We'd accept it exactly the way it was. The other side had tons of objections. We said that none of their objections was a problem, for various reasons. Then at five o'clock on the last day that you can submit objections, that was closed. The AG then has so many days to look at everything. At five o'clock on the last day they had, they overruled the objections and went with their original language.

It isn't complicated. No matter how many times you say marriage should be between one man and one woman, no matter how many times you change the words around, it still comes out marriage should be between one man and one woman. So there's not a whole lot to object to.

And it's not like you don't have precedent. These things were going on all over the nation [in 2004]. So it's not like people were ignorant. And while all of this was going on, [same-sex marriage] was on all of the media, covering about 20 percent of the news at the national level because of Massachusetts and New York and San Francisco and Oregon and all of the initiatives. Not to mention that our local press was going bonkers. It was saturated.

Then comes the objection period, where they have so long to appeal it to the [Oregon] Supreme Court. So after the AG certifies the language, they appeal it to the supreme court, and it has so many days to entertain the appeal. The supreme court said the language was fine. The supreme court could've taken as long as they wanted to decide that. They could've considered it all the way until our deadline was up for submitting signatures. We had to submit our signatures by July 2 in order to qualify for the November election. They realized the gravity of the situation and worked quickly. Now we had language, and it was May 15.

There's one more thing that the opposition can do. The other side technically could request the supreme court to reconsider its opinion. It's very unethical for any attorney to ask for reconsideration of an appeal when the court didn't even issue comments. There's nothing to reconsider. But it stalls. The lawyer for Basic Rights Oregon and Roey [Thorpe] withdrew as their attorney. Basic Rights Oregon wanted to stall the gathering of signatures. So they filed the reconsideration on their own, without an attorney, and Roey Thorpe signed it. They walked in the door with it at five minutes to five on the very last day. So it really did irritate the supreme court. At noon the next day, they just released it. That gave us five and a half weeks.

We had been putting everything in place to gather signatures. However, any petition dated prior to the certification date would be illegal. So we couldn't print anything. We couldn't circulate anything. What we could do was get our lines of communication put together and all that. But once we were able to start gathering signatures, in twenty-five years of Oregon politics, I've never ever seen anything like the response we got.

Basic Rights Oregon and the commissioners and others were convinced that there was no way we could ever gather the 130,000 signatures in five and a half weeks. Impossible. No way. Just too much work.

The five weeks were intense. But without paying anybody – we had no paid collectors – we gathered 244,000 signatures, because of the activity generated. People found out through direct mail and radio. We ran ads asking people to circulate petitions. Call this number and get a petition. We printed probably a million petition sheets and just scattered them out there. We would get between four hundred and seven hundred requests for petitions every single day. We would stay late and run them down to the post office, first class. Then we would get the petitions back ready to go. These were from individuals.

We ended up getting about 65,000 of the 244,000 [signatures] directly from churches. Oregon Family Council has been distributing voter information pamphlets through churches for twenty-five years. It's nonpartisan information. It doesn't tell anyone how to vote, but it does take the issues and gives the positions of people running for office. It also gives a real good text on issues or measures that are running. We try to provide good, educational, nonpartisan information for people.

We find that, if we provide people with information, they're educated and they vote. If they're not provided with information, they go, "Why am I going to the polls? I don't know anything about these people." We provide information on local commissioner races, state and local legislative races, mayoral races. When people walk in with our voter information, they feel that they can vote intelligently on the issues that are important to them.

Every election cycle, we distribute in the neighborhood of a quarter of a million in the primary, and another quarter of a million in the general election. Everything is free of charge, but people love the material so much that our donations take care of the cost. We distribute them through churches and Christian bookstores. And we don't go out and just drop them off. We call in advance and ask them if they want our voter information, and they tell us exactly how many they need for their congregation. Our list has 2,100 [Oregon] churches that handle our voter information in their congregations. And it's very popular. So we already had a twenty-five-year relationship [with the churches].

Yet it's not easy to get churches motivated in anything political and never has been. This is the only one that I can say has ever been easy. During political season, churches want to have a little emphasis. If we want to do a registration drive at a church, they'll take registration forms from us and be grateful. Churches want to encourage their people to be informed and vote properly.

For them to write us a check, for them to circulate a petition in their pews or in their congregation or set up a booth or whatever it is they do, that's way, way above and beyond. Of the 2,100 churches on my list that handle our voter information, under normal circumstances – on a pornography measure or informed consent or something else like that – we might be able to get 10 percent of them to do something. I had 1,200 that actually circulated this petition in their churches. There are about 3,000 churches in the state of Oregon, some of which we have no relationship with. So to the best of my knowledge, 1,200 of about 3,000 churches directly participated here. Now I know there were more than that. But that's all I can document.

[The signature collection] was so quiet because of the way it was done. The opposition kept looking for us on the streets, and they couldn't find us anywhere. So in their mind, when the day came to turn in petitions – and we did it two days early – they didn't think we made it. Their rhetoric in the press was, "There's no way they've made it. We haven't seen them anywhere. They haven't been out there."

We did no public collection whatsoever. I would agree that it's very unusual. That's why they didn't think we had them. On one day, we had fourteen full trays of mail come back. We had over 35,000 individual circulators – people who took [a petition], signed in the circulator spot on the petition, and had somebody else sign.

To follow the laws, we had printed instruction sheets that were very, very clear and specific. The majority of the initiative-petition gathering in the state of Oregon that has been brought under scrutiny as suspect has been because of paid signature gatherers. We used none. Our relationship with the secretary of state – even though he's a liberal Democrat and, in fact, in favor of same-sex marriage – and with their staff was excellent. By the time they were done going through [the signatures], we had the highest percentage of good signatures ever in the history of Oregon. Of the 244,000, they certified 208,000 on the first run-through. And the first run-through is very conservative. They throw out everything, including an additional percentage that the legislature calls for that's automatically thrown out, even if you don't look at it. After the first run-through, if you fall short, then the requirement is that they go back to the rest of it. They never got to the rest of ours. They never needed to.

We gathered 244,000 signatures in five and a half weeks, which is the largest number of signatures ever gathered for an initiative in Oregon and in the shortest period of time. Previously, the highest number of signatures had been around 160,000. And that one was filed a year and a half in advance.

Roey Thorpe was also impressed with the success of the signature gathering by the Defense of Marriage Coalition.

They had a very short time to gather a lot of signatures. To their credit, they gathered more signatures in that short time than anyone has done ever in the history of Oregon. All the predictions were that they would never make it on the ballot, and they did. Not only did they do it, they had twice as many as they needed. They hit a nerve. They spent a lot of money mailing out petitions, and they did a saturation.

We thought that they would be close in terms of the number of signatures they turned in. So our focus when they were gathering signatures was not on ramping up our campaign. It was on monitoring their activities and planning to challenge them legally. So we had people attending churches and watching. We trained them and had lots of people going to many different churches. They used check sheets – like, was the petition left unattended? In Oregon, the person signing at the bottom of the petition has to watch every signature being signed. Just, were the rules being followed? We had a handy checklist for the volunteer who wanted to go and monitor.

What we found were reports of just the worst kind of coercion. A minister in a church [during a worship service] would say, "I'd like everyone who's registered to vote to stand up." Then everybody who's registered to vote would stand up. "If you have signed this petition already, sit down." Then to the people who were still standing, they'd say, "Okay, stay standing, because we're going to bring the petition to you right now." And if you weren't going to sign that petition, you had to do so before your entire congregation. People were going to see you saying no. That's a lot of pressure. We had two reports of this.

We also had two or three different reports about faith-based food banks that were telling people that they needed to sign the petition in order to get their food. And those reports didn't come from our monitors. They came from people who went to the food banks and then called us to ask, "Can they do this? This isn't right." So that was pretty disturbing.

There were other things we had a lot of questions about. People would get a petition in the mail and mail it back to the Defense of Marriage Coalition. We were pretty concerned that sheets that weren't signed or not filled out correctly were being corrected in their office in a way that is illegal. We saw some evidence of that the day we spent monitoring the verification of signatures at the secretary of state's office.

But the volume was so huge that we realized it was pointless to continue to contest it. We would've had to get more than half of the signatures thrown out. We could have pursued that and asked more questions, but we did not. In the end, there isn't any mechanism that says, if the state finds that some [objections are] true, then all of the signatures are invalid. Instead, there's a system of random validation of signatures. It's not like every signature gets looked at. And the volume was so huge that it just seemed like a waste of our efforts. It felt like more denial on our part. I thought, let's just go ahead here. We need to ramp up this campaign and ramp it up now.

The Measure 36 Campaign

Tim Nashif described the campaign run by the Defense of Marriage Coalition once the initiative was certified for the November ballot.

There were some interesting things about our media campaign. I went on a program called "Town Hall," which is a well-known Oregon program on KATU, the ABC affiliate [in Portland]. They

123

line up key people on one side and every one else on the other side, and they have a moderator. They do this town hall and go back and forth. It's a great program.

I sat down, and right next to me were a couple of guys I understood to be gay. And I'm thinking, they're sitting on the wrong side. They put the supporters of Measure 36 on one side, and those against Measure 36 on the other side. And so I'm thinking these guys must be sitting on the wrong side. The debate is all about benefits. Steve Dunn, the moderator, goes to these two guys, and it turns out they're supporters of Measure 36. They are adamant supporters of Measure 36. They live together and have been partners for a number of years. They said, "Look, we believe marriage should be between one man and one woman. They keep talking about all these benefits, and that offends us. Because we already have all the benefits they say we don't have as a couple. All we had to do to get visitation rights was this one piece of paper. It took us five minutes and didn't cost any money. We have our pension benefits. We have wills. Most attorneys even tell married people they're supposed to do those things. So everybody is doing these things anyway. We don't understand your saying that we can't do this. You're being disingenuous and dishonest, because those benefits are available to us, and we can prove it."

I had never before seen this couple. The news media found them. They live in Eugene, and one of them is the brother of an Oregon state representative. I asked if they would do a TV spot for us. It was really cool. They said, "We are in favor of Measure 36. And here's why. We've got these benefits and that benefit. And we believe that marriage should be between one man and one woman." They were 100 percent volunteer, and both of them professionals. One works with and sells RVs all over the country. The other one worked at Sears for fifteen years.

I also had an ad with a deputy superintendent of public instruction in Oregon, now retired. He was also a principal for twenty-five years. He said that same-sex marriage would be confusing and harmful because of the way it would affect schools. He said it would be harmful because it would bring confusion into the schools.

We had a report out of Massachusetts done by National Public Radio. It was all about sex education in Massachusetts schools since the legalization of same-sex marriage there. It talked about how gay sex is now being taught in Massachusetts schools. It interviewed a teacher who teaches gay sex, and how she introduces concepts of gay sex in sex education and health courses. "Can a woman and a woman have sex? Well of course they can. They use toys." And she has graphs on the toys.

The whole time that this was going on [in Multnomah County], we were being told, look, nothing in same-sex marriage is going to force churches [in Oregon] to do this or that. Yet a Catholic school in Eugene was being sued for $550,000 by a lesbian couple whose child applied to attend there. Homosexuality is against the teaching of the church. Therefore, the school's administration said, "We're sorry, but we can't accept the child into the school." So the question came up, what if same-sex marriage was legal and a religious school refused a child with gay parents? The whole game plan is changed. What if a rural school district in southern Oregon doesn't want gay sex in their "diversity education"? Well, there will have to be a policy or there will be lawsuits flying for "diversity in education" in all of these things. And it will be forced upon school districts.

So those were points we made in our media campaign. Are we concerned about it today [after Measure 36 passed]? No. Would we be concerned about it if same-sex marriage was put on the same platform with heterosexual marriage? Absolutely, we would be concerned about it, because how could you go any other direction? It's impossible. You have to.

So that was our concern. What kind of a confusing message does this send to young people? Whoever brings this to the forefront – whether it's a polygamist, whether it's two cousins that want to marry, whether it's two men and a woman who want to marry, whether it's two people of the same sex – anytime you put it on the same plane as marriage between one man and one woman, once you've redefined marriage, you've basically undefined it. You've made it of no effect. You've opened a floodgate. How do you draw the line?

Marriage has never been applied to anybody and everybody. To say that it should be does what a lot of gay activist groups really want. If you read their Web sites, you understand clearly that the real activist groups would like there not to be any marriage.

It's never been about benefits, because the benefits are available. People don't want to take benefits away from anyone. Benefits can be applied across the board, and not only to gays. They can be applied to a grandmother whose grandson takes care of her in her later days. They can be applied to two sisters who live together, to widows or widowers who live together, a brother and a sister who live together. Anyone who is restricted from the marriage entity could have legal benefits, and that would help families. Who's against that? Nobody's against that. I can't find anyone on either side of the aisle that's really against that. I find some businesses are concerned with over-applying benefits and what that will do to their insurance costs and those kinds of things. But benefits cannot be restricted to just two same-sex people, no matter how they try to wind it up and put it together. Doing so heads in the direction of undefining marriage, which is extremely harmful to families. If you said to a child, "You no longer need a mom and a dad," I think that child, and most children, would object.

The same thing happened with no-fault divorce. If you said to a kid, "Look, we are going to make it easier for your mom and dad to split up," that kid might say, "Wait a minute. I don't want you to make it easier for my mom and dad to split up. I want my family to be together." We went the same direction when we loosened the divorce laws.

Kelly Clark, the attorney for the Defense of Marriage Coalition, offered a different point of view about one aspect of its media campaign.

A highlight, or lowlight, of the campaign came when the Measure 36 proponents decided to bring children into the discussion. You know, "Social science research shows children do best in homes with two opposite-sex parents." That was a theme of the campaign. I always thought that was tricky.

We had to argue that in the court case, because of the question of what could possibly be the legislative justification for excluding same-sex couples from marriage. Our answer was, the main reason the state continues to be involved in licensing private relationships is out of concern for the procreation and rearing of children. That's the historic justification. And there's plenty of social science research to show that that's a rational conclusion. It's not saying that gays are bad parents. It's not saying anything except that a rational legislature could believe that children are best off in the tried and true family model. The legislature could decide that without being unconstitutionally discriminatory.

Now, it's one thing when you say that in a context of defending the legislative rationale for a statute. It's a very precise, narrow legal argument that you're making. It's a possible justification for a legislative distinction. "Judge, you don't even have to believe the studies. You don't have to agree with them. You just have to believe that a rational legislature could."

It's very dangerous and difficult to go from that and make it into a campaign ad that says children are best off in opposite-sex homes. Because it invites the suggestion that you're saying that gays aren't good parents and aren't capable human beings and all that sort of stuff. I was worried about that, when the Measure 36 campaign began to run ads featuring teachers saying, "I don't want to have to teach gay sex education in classrooms. This is going to be confusing to children." I was afraid that it had gone too far and that there would be a perception that this was an attack on gays. The other side jumped on that very quickly and said, yes, that's exactly what it is. "The homophobia that we always knew was there is now surfacing."

Roey Thorpe offered the perspective of Basic Rights Oregon on the Measure 36 campaign.

Anytime there's a ballot measure campaign here, it brings out the best in our community. People really step up. They help in every way that they can. They come out of the woodwork with expressions of support.

One thing that makes Oregon special is that, because we've had so many ballot measure campaigns, there's not so much of a division between gay and straight people. Many more straight people are aware of gay rights issues here than they are in other places. And our organization is much more integrated, gay and straight, than probably any state gay rights organization in the country, even more than California. It's really pretty amazing.

But I was unaware of the extent to which the other side would lie. I say that very intentionally. They just lied. They sent out glossy brochures saying there'd be increased numbers of abortions if same-sex marriage were legal. They sent out glossy brochures saying homosexuality would be taught in kindergarten and that it had already begun in Massachusetts. I was really surprised that they would go to that length here. In fact, I don't think it helped them. I think it hurt them. Nonetheless, I was surprised at their dishonesty.

Throughout the entire campaign, a lot of churches gave money and put signs on their front lawns, sometimes big ones, that were very visible. They successfully made this into people of faith versus the gays, people of faith defending America's traditional values – despite the many, many endorsements we had from people of faith and from churches and faith organizations. Somehow those voices never made it to a volume where they were heard over the other side. That's a problem for us in the future that we're trying to address. So the churches were extremely, extremely visible.

But let me be clear. I'm only concerned about [what the churches did] from a political perspective. I'm not concerned about the propriety of it. Do I think that the message itself was reprehensible? Yes. But the part regarding propriety that concerns me has to do with whether those churches were motivated at all by wanting to reelect the President. I do feel that it's appropriate for them to weigh in on a ballot measure, and we encourage churches to weigh in as well. So I'm not going to be a hypocrite and say we should do it and they shouldn't. But if there was any motivation having to do with the presidential election, I think that is inappropriate. It's inappropriate for all churches.

Now, I don't actually know how much that was the case [in Oregon]. In fact, my gut feeling tells me that, as much as I believe there was a national strategy to increase the President's chances of winning by bringing this issue onto the ballot, I don't actually believe in my gut that's what motivated evangelical churches here. I don't know about other places. Here, I believe that this genuinely fits in with their value system. I don't agree with that, but I don't suspect them of wanting to reelect the President.

In fact, in Oregon, we're suspicious about national politics and government in general. I suspect that some of those churches were uncomfortable with the idea that their commitment on this issue could be used to influence the presidential election. My guess is that some of those folks found that offensive.

Do I think there's a general erosion of the separation of church and state and that it's a very intentional erosion from the right? Yes, and it very much concerns me. I just don't know that

I think .... There are a lot of people who called us up, for instance, to say, "Hey, I know how you can really get back at the people who passed this amendment. Do you know that *churches* were involved in it?" "Well, yes, *where* were *you*?" They say, "That's illegal." And I say, "Well, no it's *not*."

Yes, that's a serious problem, and perhaps this issue played out nationally and in other states in a way that fit into a strategy. But I don't believe that churches speaking out on *this* issue in Oregon conform to that model, as much as I find it personally offensive that anyone would say that their God believes in discriminating against a group of people.

And as much as I'm tired of this sanctimonious crap about – you know, this is what God wants, and about how God loves you, but why don't you just change – I have a neighbor who said to me, "*You* could get married. You *could* get married. Just marry a *man*." She had a sign in her yard that said, "Yes on 36," and I went and talked to her. That's what she said to me, and I find that completely offensive. But I don't think it's wrong, and I don't think it's wrong for churches to weigh in on social policy issues.

Aftermath

Roey Thorpe reflected on the popular rejection of marriage rights for same-sex couples in Oregon.

Is there anything we could have done differently? We sent out canvassers and talked personally to over a quarter of a million people during this campaign, either on the phone or on people's doorsteps. Which is huge, because Oregon has two and a half million people.

When we first started out, we were determined that our message would be about marriage. [Same-sex marriage] was a new idea for a lot of people concerning something very traditional and very much taken for granted. But everyone who was a savvy political thinker said, really, the key to this is that you've got to talk about it being a constitutional amendment, and this doesn't belong in our constitution.

The truth is, people were actually more moved on the issue itself. One thing that surprised us at the end, when we were doing polling late in the campaign to figure out where we were, was the extent to which people had moved on the issue of marriage itself, [especially] once they had a conversation about it. If we had known how much people would move, we would have emphasized that more and earlier. All of the momentum in this campaign was on our side. If we had had more time, I think we would've done much better.

But mostly what I think is, if I had it to do over again, I would have believed much earlier that this was going to get on the ballot. Like people all over the country, I was surprised at how it managed to get there. If I had believed that earlier, I would have started fund raising earlier. We would have had a different campaign plan. It would have been longer, and we would have had more money earlier. We could've started doing more education earlier.

Whether I could have convinced anyone else that it would actually make it on the ballot, I'm not sure. I know that we got a significant amount of national funding, as well as individuals around the country who helped us. But a lot of it came fairly late. People had to be convinced. We just didn't have the money to launch a big media campaign that started earlier.

In Oregon, we do all of our voting by mail. So we made a strategic decision to have our ads up, and most of our mailers happening, while people had their ballots. We did a little bit earlier, some radio advertising, and a little bit of television. We might have stretched that out more or started earlier if we had the money and realized how much people would move on the issue itself.

The other thing I would do as an organization would be to make sure that we built better relationships with people-of-color organizations. Because the issue of whether this was a civil rights matter became more of a question than it ever needed to. The Defense of Marriage Coalition was very clever about how they did that. They had only one person who spoke for their campaign, and it was Georgene Rice. She's a very compelling speaker, a smart woman, and lovely – and African-American. She said the most absurd and ridiculous things, but she said them with such certainty, like, "These people have *never* been denied a seat at a lunch counter. This is not a civil rights issue." As though civil rights began and ended with lunch counters! There have been many civil rights struggles in this country. Some of them have involved African-Americans. Yet what was said here was just silly. But you know, she said it, and we didn't have people prepared to stand up and challenge her. And we should have.

Now, those relationships built during the campaign, and we're trying to continue them. Mind you, it's not like their side really had those strong relationships either. They had Georgene and a couple of conservative African-American ministers from the downtown Baptist churches. That's not an overwhelming number, but we didn't have any more than that.

I believe that if the [Measure 36] campaign could have been won, we'd've won it. I do believe that, as much as I still think there's plenty of things about our own campaign we would want to do better next time. We had the strongest campaign in the country, the best funded, the most expert. We had tremendous support from national organizations, and also from Oregon. We have people here who have worked on so many campaigns, who really knew what they were doing. We ran a full-out campaign.

On the other hand, their side spent more, just this one time, than Lon Mabon [and the Oregon Citizens Alliance] spent in its entire history of antigay campaigns. In fact, their campaign spent more than all of the other antigay campaigns around the country in 2004 combined. They had over $2.2 million in reported contributions. And I think that there were other rather vast in-kind contributions that weren't reported.

By comparison, our budget was a little over $2.8 million. In 2000, we defeated an antigay ballot measure. We spent $1.4 million, and the other side spent $330,000. And that $330,000 is from when the petitioning started, about a year before the election, and all through the campaign. We outspent them like five to one.

In this case, we did outspend them, but not by much. And if you figure that you really need to outspend your opponent to educate people on an issue that's new to them and does involve a change in how people think about something really fundamental, then, we did pretty darn well. And there's no way that we could have raised, like, $10 million. There's just no way.

Tim Nashif offered reasons for the success of Measure 36.

People were saddened and angered that marriage licenses in Oregon were given out [to same-sex couples] without any debate. They were flabbergasted by it. They could not believe they didn't have a voice in the process, and that these four [Multnomah County commissioner] women would be so arrogant to do that. That was one reason.

Another reason is that people do not want same-sex marriage. Period. They just don't want it. If I'm a mother or a father, I don't say, "Boy, I've got three children, and I hope some day that I find out that one of them is gay." That's the reality of life. Moms don't do that. Moms don't say, "I just can't wait to find out some day that – yea! – I have a gay child." They don't think that way. Now gays may think that way. But mothers in general don't think that way. Fathers don't think that way. They want their children to grow up, they want them to get married, they want them to have children, they want them to have families.

There are a lot of parents that wake up one day and find out they have a gay child. Now their responsibility to that child is to support that child in every way they can. And they wouldn't be good parents if they weren't supportive and caring, even if they didn't agree with the lifestyle. Because it's their child. But they don't wish for it. They don't hope for it. They don't try to make it happen.

So when you start saying that we're going to put same-sex marriage relationships up front, we're going to teach same-sex education in the schools, we're going to reserve somebody's decision as to what their lifestyle will be and what their sexual orientation is – we want them to withhold their decision until they get older so they can experience all aspects of it – you scare the living daylights out of parents. You really do, because they don't want their kids to be gay. They'll accept them if they are, but they're not wishing for it.

I think that's the crux of this. That's what's being missed – how Americans really feel about this.

Another thing I found out from my research is that, ten or fifteen years ago, gays were saying, "We just want to come out of the closet." People today don't see them in the same light as they did a decade ago. They see them as being extreme activists, a lot of them, because they keep going after more.

So people don't believe gays are going to stop with marriage. They think their agenda is going to continue. People are not so naïve, at this point, to think that once same-sex marriage is established, there will be no more need for a gay lobby. It's not the way politics works. It doesn't matter if you have an issue you need anymore. You gotta do it to keep the ball rolling. You gotta keep your issue alive. It's part of the problem when you win and are successful at something. You just don't fold up shop and go home and say, "Oh great! We did this, and we're done." You don't want to put yourself out of business. Some people might do that out of integrity. They might say, "Hey look, I'm done with this, and I'm happy to be done with it. And God bless America." But somebody else is going to pick up that ball and run with it.

And when you dig into it, you find out that there's a huge difference in mentality between a gay activist and a gay person. There's a split in their own group, and they're very concerned about it, because not every gay person thinks that they should have gay marriage or that you should go down the road of gay marriage. Some gays don't want to get married. They understand each other, that this particular relationship is fine, but it may last for only two or three years, because it's the nature of their relationships. They are not intended for a lifetime. It's not the nature of their culture. I'm not going to say it's not the nature of everyone in their culture. There's a diversity there. But for the most part, if you look at the statistics, it's clear. So I think there's a split in their own thinking.

Kelly Clark provided an alternative rationale to explain why Oregon voters approved Measure 36.

I have a hunch about these ballot measures. When it comes to gay rights, at least in Oregon, whoever is perceived as being on the offense loses. So Lon Mabon and the Oregon Citizens Alliance lost [in the 1990s], because they were perceived as being on offense.

In some ways, unspoken and even perhaps unrecognized, this was a campaign to make the other guys appear to be on offense. Ballot Measure 36 supporters were continually running on what happened in Multnomah County and how outrageous it was as a matter of public policy and process.

One of my favorite catch phrases was, "Why is it that those on the other side don't think the people of Oregon are smart enough or fair enough or wise enough to decide this question? They want to take it away from you and give it to the judges." So our side was saying, it's the gay community that's on the offense here, trying, without hearings, to change things instantly.

The other side was saying the same thing in retrospect. One of their *best* campaign ads was a soccer-mom-type woman saying, "I don't really know what I think about gay marriage, but I don't think we should use the Constitution to hurt people." Again, it's those guys that are on offense. We're not. We're just being on defense.

But there had been so much publicity surrounding what happened in Multnomah County. This is a liberal state, but when the *Oregonian* calls for the resignation or recall of Multnomah County commissioners, that's just stunning. I was in legal seminars where Portland lawyers to the left of center would come up to me and say, "What were they thinking?" [Gays] started off so badly that the Measure 36 folks could keep reminding Oregonians of it: "We got here because a group of rogue Multnomah County commissioners took the law into their own hands and thought you were too stupid to decide this on your own." I'm not sure that the 57 percent of the people who supported [Measure 36] ever really got past that starting point. My assessment, then, is that gays were perceived as being on offense [in Multnomah County], and so the people said, "No, we're not prepared for this yet."

I have said to my friends in the gay community, you guys would have been a whole lot better off if you had gone back a year and run your own ballot measure that had the top twenty benefits of marriage that you want extended to same-sex couples. You know, the right to visit each other in the hospital, the right to intestate succession, the right to make medical-care decisions. Whatever your top twenty are, take those to Oregonians and say, "Prove us right. Prove that you're not biased against homosexuals. Prove your basic decency and fairness. Look at these. Don't they make sense?" That would've been a whole lot smarter move than what you did. And I honestly believe, knowing something about the way Oregon voters think, that a well-run campaign by the gay community would have done very, very well in this state.

I understand, even if I haven't lived it out, that for somebody like me to say, "Take ten years and make your case," that's a long time to be denied justice if you're on the other side. But I ask this question, if they had gone out and run the ballot measure that I suggested, their "Top 20" Bill of Rights, win or lose, would they be better off than they are now? My answer is, they couldn't be worse off.

As a community, we couldn't be worse off if they had done that. In fact, we would be substantially further down the road toward some consensus on this, because the gay community would have said to the population, "We know you think that there's some secret gay agenda. There is no secret gay agenda. We just want justice. Here's what it looks like in twenty ways."

Roey Thorpe, the person most responsible for the Multnomah County strategy, responded to Kelly Clark's analysis.

This is one of the key things I learned. I don't think I knew it going into this. [Kelly Clark] assumes that what marriage is about for us is those top twenty rights. And that is *not* what it's about. I might have been more inclined to believe in a strategy like that before all this happened.

I'll tell you a story. What you should know is that I'm a person who never wanted to get married. I did when I was a kid, but as an adult, I've not wanted to do that. I've never lived with any of my partners until the current one. We've been together for three years. I would not have been the person who proposed marriage in our relationship. But we got married at our house on the Saturday after the marriages started.

My partner invited her whole family, who all live here in Portland, and her friends. I invited my friends. My most important people are scattered all over the country, and there was no time for them to be here. Our wedding was very emotional, as were all of the weddings I observed.

Her family has always been so supportive of me. They have treated me like a member of the family since they met me. They've included me in every way that you could be included. It's remarkable. Not only are we both women, but I'm a gay rights activist. That's not a very easy thing to integrate into your family. But her family has not batted an eye.

My partner's sister came up to me after the wedding and said, "Welcome to the family." It was a profound moment for me. What I realized was that, although I didn't feel any more like a member of the family than I had before, for her, that ritual, that wedding was a rite of passage. And no list of twenty rights gives you that. I had not even been aware of that before.

I'll give you another example. Her eighty-five-year-old grandmother was there with her boyfriend [she giggles]. She's about as big as a minute. She's a tiny little lady, all pink and white. She came to our wedding, and we talked about it afterward. She said, "You know, it was just like every other wedding." She was surprised by that.

Well, the year before, I had invited her to come to Basic Rights Oregon's annual dinner. My partner and I had bought a table, and we invited her whole family to come. She said, "You know, dear, I just don't know if I would be comfortable." I said, "That's fine. I understand. No problem." But I resolved that I would ask her every year. So this year, in October, after our wedding, I asked her again. She said, "I would love to." And I said, "So what changed for you?" I thought her answer was going to be something like, "I came to your wedding, and I realized that gay people are okay. I got more comfortable." Instead, what she said was, "Well, dear, it's a family thing now." So today I'm her granddaughter-in-law, or whatever you call it. And now for her, it's something that I'm doing. So she'll go, because it's about family.

This is the most profound thing that I learned. It's also the most profoundly painful thing, because – I don't even know if I can say this without crying – it means that we aren't family without it, [she does cry as she says] and I don't think we realize that until it happens. It's so heartbreaking, because ... [composing herself].

I can really make light of it, like all these staunch, fifty-something lesbian and gay male couples who said to me, "I don't need marriage. We're not going to get married. What's all this about? Why is this the direction of the movement?" And those were not the people who were standing in line to get married the first week. They were the people who were there the second week. And all of them have said that they just didn't know ... [she begins crying again]. That pain is something that we are not in touch with. And we can't be. Because in order to live your life, you have to deny that pain. In order to have any kind of happiness, you can't think about it all the time.

Our movement's been remarkable in helping people deal with that, and helping us think it through, and helping us believe and support the idea that we can have a ceremony in our church or that we can have a domestic partnership or we can have something and it doesn't matter what other people think because we know what we have. But you know what – it matters.

So what I say to Kelly Clark is, then, let's see *you* have just those twenty rights, and let's see *you* not be married, and let's see *you* have to deal with the fact that people don't believe your relationship counts or that your love is as good or as true.

There's a story I tell that I hadn't really thought much about until I started [at Basic Rights Oregon]. Before I worked here, I was the director of a big child-care center in upstate New York. There was a woman I worked with there, in the mid-1990s, when half of my friends had died from AIDS. It was a horrible time. She was a woman who had just lost her husband tragically and unexpectedly. They'd been married for over twenty years and her youngest child had just gone off to college. Finally, all the kids were out of the house, that kind of thing. Then her husband died in a plane crash, and it was really, really sad. When she finally returned to work, she came into my office every single day. She would just break down and cry, and I would listen to her. We would cry together and talk it through. Finally, one day she said to me, "I've been meaning to ask you something, Roey. Do you feel bad when your person dies?" Like, do "you people" feel bad? And I couldn't believe it. I just couldn't believe she was asking me that. I realized in that moment that, all along, even though I was the person she had chosen to confide in, she believed I was a little bit less human, on a really fundamental level. And she didn't even see what was offensive about asking me that question.

The reason I've told that story so much in the past year is that that is what this issue is about. We can say it's about all kinds of things. But that is really what it's about. It's about, is our love as true? Are we as fully human? Are we as worthy of being part of people's families? Are we as deserving? On the most fundamental level, that's what it's about.

So for the people who don't think that marriage is the right direction for this movement, or that it's too much too soon, I

137

understand that as an intellectual exercise. But, man, the reason that this is the issue now is that, as far as we have come, there's a fundamental challenge that we have not made to people's assumptions about us.

I would argue the same thing about the African-American civil rights movement. As far as that movement came in terms of determining legal rights, there are fundamental racist threads that run through our culture and assumptions that people have that are not challenged. And for us, this is that challenge.

When asked whether the Multnomah County/Measure 36 experience offered other lessons, Roey Thorpe added the following.

I never predicted how emotional all of this would be. When we started and were doing all this strategizing, what was remarkable was the way all the people in our legal group and I and the other strategists never talked about our own relationships. We never talked about whether or not we would get married. We never talked about the personal end of it. We only talked about the rights and the political strategy, and I just didn't know.

I didn't even know, until I saw what happened in San Francisco, that people would even want to get married. One of the things we talked about here was, how are we going to find people who want to get married? We didn't know that. It's so funny now in retrospect. What we realized in watching California – and thank God for us being able to watch that – was that we thought, "Oh my gosh, the county clerk here doesn't perform marriages." So we were, like, where are people going to get married? Who is going to marry them? What is going to happen? So we actually set up a very sophisticated operation at the county office, letting people know everything that they needed to do to get married.

Yet when we were setting all that up and preparing everything, we had no idea about the emotion that it was going to bring up. I remember standing there during the first weddings. The room was crowded with press and couples' families. It was over at the Hilton. I was standing there with the folks from the ACLU, and we were going to have a press conference right afterwards. I had my notes in hand. I mean it was, like, all business. And that wedding started, and I started crying and could not stop. And there was not a dry eye in the house. The press, everybody, was just completely in tears. We were literally, like, just blown away.

We would have these staff meetings at ten o'clock, every single night, for the first couple of weeks [after the weddings started], and the whole BRO staff would tell stories and just sob.

We have this photo and caption still hanging on our office door. It's a picture from the *Oregonian*, and there's this man with a sign that says, "Congratulations! 54 years ago, I would have been in line with you. With luck I may be in line in 2004, too." The caption beneath the photo says, "Nelson Jones, seventy-four, of Portland greets gay and lesbian couples waiting in line this morning for Multnomah County marriage licenses with a sign that refers to his forty-one-year relationship with a partner who died twelve years ago. Jones said he and his current partner hope to marry this year."

At a staff meeting, they handed me this photo and said, "Roey, read the caption out loud!" I looked at the photo and began reading the caption, and started crying and couldn't stop. Everyone started laughing, because they knew that there was no way. . . . They had all done the same thing with each other, "Read this out loud! Read this out loud!" There was no way to get through it without just crying and crying. It was so emotional.

What happened with those marriages, the reason they were so emotional, was not only that weddings are emotional and beautiful, but that people were experiencing for the first time what it felt like to be equal. That was really a big part of it. They felt different. And no matter what this ballot measure says, and no matter what happens, people exposed themselves to a kind of vulnerability and put themselves out there in this really courageous personal way. They dared to say, "I'm going to do this because I deserve it." And it changed people, like in the way people stood up when their friends and loved ones were dying of AIDS, who said, "We don't deserve this. We deserve better than this."

And there's no going back from that sort of personal change. No going back from it. Of course it matters tremendously if we have a federal constitutional amendment. And of course it matters tremendously that this terrible ballot measure passed here. But even though legally we are behind where we were a year ago, we are ahead.

When I listen to people in other states talk about the apathy of their lesbian and gay community around marriage or anything else, I think that will never be the case here. Because we have changed here. The only other people who understand it are the folks in San Francisco. Maybe in New Paltz and New Mexico, too. I haven't spoken with them. But I do think there's power in the mass of people [who married]. It really made a huge difference.

And that's why lobbying the legislature for a civil unions bill now is so anticlimactic. A year ago, two years ago, it would have been fantastic. It would have been jubilation. Now, it's a really nice swimming pool that's separate. Now it's "gays only." It's separate and unequal. Yes, it would be a step forward, given what we have. But it's a step backward from where we are emotionally and where we are in terms of our own belief in ourselves and our self-worth.

That actually is the position of this organization. Civil unions are a step forward, but they are not a goal. They are not what we deserve. They're less than what they deserve. Yes, we support them because we're practical. But we don't believe in them or embrace them, because they are discriminatory.

Kelly Clark offered an assessment of how receptive the Oregon Legislature would be to granting civil union or domestic-partnership benefits to same-sex couples after the passage of Measure 36.

There's certainly nothing in Measure 36 that precludes [civil unions]. They are an option, just as they would have been before Measure 36. Someone could go to the legislature, and it could extend some or all of the benefits of marriage to same-sex couples. Politically, though, it's unlikely the legislature would do something like that now.

I was asked to go down [to Salem, the state capital] and brief the House and Senate Republican caucus, right after [the trial court's] ruling came down. I went into the caucus room, and there were probably forty Republican members of the assembly, both senators and representatives. Even then, and this was back in May or June [2004], it felt to me like the consensus reaction I got was, "Over my dead body will I vote for civil unions."

[Oregon has] a very conservative Republican house and now a solidly Democrat and solidly liberal senate, and a thoughtful, liberal governor. So it'll be very interesting to see what happens. I just don't see much moving out of [the 2005] session.

My personal belief is that this has gone way too fast. We need some tilling of the soil. We need some time for this to settle, and for people to get used to the idea. The average citizen just needs some time.

I put myself in that situation. I was totally taken aback by [what happened in Multnomah County]. Reporters started asking me early on, "Well, what's your position on all of this?" "I don't know! I grew up a Southerner, and I'm sort of conservative. I know I believe in traditional marriage, but I have never really even thought about gay marriage. Give me some time to figure all this out. I don't have anything against gays. I don't see why they shouldn't be able to visit each other in the hospital, and have tax advantages, and all of that. So I'm a big puddle of logical mass, like I think many people in the middle of the political spectrum are. Give me some time to sort this out."

When pressed on the question of "What now?" Roey Thorpe speculated about the political prospects of legislative relief.

I don't know honestly. It's really hard to predict. It depends on how much visibility we can bring to the importance of these issues, saying, "Look, we've been dealt a terrible wrong here, and you need to do what you can to repair it."

We can all look back at how "separate but equal" was the wrong thing under Jim Crow. It's weird to be in a situation where we are actually advocating for that and to be a part of wanting to create something like that. The hard thing for us is that we don't really want it. But we recognize that, for many couples, it offers some protections that they really need right now. We hope that the disparity between what that offers and what marriage offers is a point of education that will let us move forward.

That is particularly true if the same-sex marriages that already occurred are deemed to be valid by the court. Then there's a contrast there. What's the difference between these two couples? Clearly, nothing. So we'll see.

It's sobering to be in that position. There's none of the jubilation of the marriages. It's a resignation to what our political possibilities are at this moment.

In April 2005, the Oregon Supreme Court ruled that Multnomah County didn't have the authority to issue marriage licenses to same-sex couples and nullified all of the gay and lesbian marriages performed there (*Li v. State*), just as its California counterpart did eight months earlier.

What is more, the Oregon Legislature did not pass a civil unions bill during 2005, despite a strong endorsement of the measure by Governor Ted Kulongoski. The Beaver State legislature is in session for six months once every two years.

SIX

New York

IN MAY 2003, Jason West was elected mayor of the Village of New Paltz, about seventy miles north of New York City. In two prior attempts at public office, campaigns for the state assembly in 2000 and 2002, West lost by large margins. But getting out the vote of students from the State University of New York College at New Paltz, the twenty-six-year-old Green Party candidate achieved his first electoral success in the mayoral race.

Soon after taking office, West asked Spencer McLaughlin, the village attorney, to investigate whether New York State mayors had the capacity to preside over same-sex marriages. McLaughlin wrote a memorandum indicating that state law was ambiguous and that the mayor's judgment would determine the matter in the final analysis. Mayor West continued the story:

> I had Spencer's memo and, reading the law myself, thought it crystal-clear that [same-sex marriage] was already legal [in New York].
>
> I started talking to [lesbian and gay] couples in the summer of 2003 and found a handful of people who might be interested in marriage, were it legal. None of them had really committed to it yet, because it had never been a possibility for them before. It's a hard enough decision for straight couples to get married, for whom it's always an option. So these couples who had never had the choice took a while to think about it.
>
> In January, my friends Billiam and Jeffrey said, "Yes, let's do it. We want to be the first couple you marry." So we planned it for the summer of 2004, when the weather would be nice, and with lots of advance notice to friends and family, like a traditional wedding.

But national events picked up so fast in January and February. [Mayor] Gavin [Newsom] started the marriages in San Francisco. Then New Mexico started issuing licenses, but got closed down. The media indicated that San Francisco would be shut down, too. Then, [President] Bush, in late February, announced his endorsement of the Federal Marriage Amendment. So it looked like things were swinging in the other direction.

I spoke to Billiam and Jeffrey and a few others. We felt an urgency to do it then. We couldn't wait any longer. We needed to show there was another community supporting this. We wanted to expand and push the movement. So I asked the town clerk to issue licenses, and she refused, saying she had gotten direct orders from the [New York State] Department of Health not to give marriage licenses to same-sex couples.

I remember looking for lawyers. That was one holdup. We couldn't use the village attorney, because the village might be bankrupted with lawsuits. So I spent a week talking to law firms and ended up waiting on Heller, Ehrman, White and McAuliffe to see if their partners were willing to take on more pro bono work.

And then Bush made his announcement. Two days later, Heller, Ehrman said yes. So then we got on the phone to the four couples who had committed and told them, "Tomorrow, at noon, we're going to do this." We didn't give much press lead time, because we were afraid of a preliminary injunction. We wanted to get people married first, and then deal with the courts.

So the timing was mostly brought on by the urgency of the movement nationally. Otherwise, it would have been in the summer of 2004.

Thus, on Friday, February 27, Mayor West officiated at the weddings of twenty-four same-sex couples. Less than a week later, Ulster County District Attorney Donald A. Williams charged West with multiple misdemeanor counts of solemnizing marriages without a license.

Mayor West described the public reaction to his decision.

The Village of New Paltz itself is overwhelmingly supportive [of same-sex marriage]. On less than twenty-four hours' notice, the weddings drew a crowd of 500 or 600 people, in a village of

6,000. A week later, when I was arraigned and had a ten-minute court appearance, word got around that I was going to court, and there was a crowd of between 1,000 and 1,500 supporters. The letters and e-mails I got were like ten-to-one in favor. So in the New Paltz community, it's 95 percent support.

Beyond that, some people were opposed. Many I spoke to had mixed reactions. Family members of mine, for example, are evangelical Christians. They say that they're personally against same-sex marriage. They don't think it's right. But they would never do anything to stop it, because they don't think it's their business to tell other people how to marry.

That was one of the most surprising reactions I heard, people making a distinction for themselves between church and state, especially evangelical Christians, who are supposed to be Bush supporters, and saying, "Religiously, I'm opposed. In terms of public policy, I think it's fine."

I have an uncle who's a prison guard and whose buddies, the other prison guards, made fun of him a lot. He'd walk out to his car after work, and they'd start singing "Here Comes the Bride" and adding words about New Paltz. They'd ask my uncle, "So what is it? Is he gay? What's he doing this for?" "No, he's straight as an arrow. He just thinks this is the right thing to do." Then, they'd say, "Right on. We don't think it's right. But he's standing up for his convictions. We need more politicians like that."

So I don't trust the polls that I hear about this. While they say that X percent of Americans are opposed to same-sex marriage, they don't make a distinction between personal religious opinion and whether there should be public policy on it. There are few people I've met who say both that they're personally opposed to same-sex marriage and that we need laws to prevent it. Most people recognize it's a personal choice and they don't have the right to interfere in other people's lives.

To the question of, if that were true, then why had he and two New Paltz village trustees been the only public officials in New York State to take this step, Mayor West responded:

Only elected officials of the Green Party took action on this. That partisan issue is why no other officials did anything. Other mayors and town officials I've met won't take the stand because they worry about their own political careers. Or they've been told not to take a stand because it would upset the chances of other people in their party to win office.

Around the time that Bush made his announcement, the mayor of Schenectady [near Albany, the state capital] said that he didn't see any problem with this. As soon as he got the okay from the city attorney, he was going forward to marry same-sex couples. I asked folks in the Empire State Pride Agenda [New York's statewide lesbian and gay organization] about what happened to that. They told me he got a call from someone higher up in his party who said, "Like hell you're going to marry same-sex couples. Because if you do, you won't run for mayor again. You're not going to make this a campaign issue."

It's the same for Democrats and Republicans. [Republican New York] Governor [George] Pataki was angling for a cabinet position in the second Bush term. He couldn't take a stand on same-sex marriage, because doing so would close off one of his political options. He needed to be a moderate Republican to run in New York State, and a right-wing Republican to be a member of the Bush administration.

It's the same for [New York State Attorney General] Elliott Spitzer, who's the presumptive Democratic nominee for governor [in 2006]. He didn't want to take a position on this because he seeks higher office and doesn't want this to be a campaign issue. For two years, organizations like Lambda Legal [Defense and Education Fund] and the Empire State Pride Agenda asked Spitzer for an opinion about whether same-sex marriage was legal in New York State. And he simply refused to take a stand. But within one week of the marriages in New Paltz, he had a decision out. [Spitzer determined that New York State law does not permit same-sex marriages to be performed in the state, but that the law does require gay and lesbian marriages that are legally performed elsewhere to be recognized in New York.] So it was something he obviously was dragging his feet on until we forced him to take the stand he didn't otherwise want to do.

So the reason no one else in New York performed same-sex weddings is because of state and national politics. Party operatives made sure that their local officials didn't make any noise on this issue. There were some exceptions, such as Mayor John Shields of Nyack [about twenty-five miles north of New York City], who is openly gay and a Democrat. Some Democrats in safe legislative districts publicly favor same-sex marriage, and I was even given an award by the New York Senate Democratic Conference. But it's all quiet and behind the scenes.

Taking a position on the issue is actually a lot safer than doing something about it. Platitudes are easy. Action is tough. Too many politicians are willing to concede the issue because they don't think it's winnable right now. I think that's tactically inaccurate.

Yet West's bold move came with a price, in the form of criminal prosecution. But in July 2005, the Ulster County district attorney dropped all charges against Mayor West, stating that a trial would be needless and divisive (Medina 2005).

When asked whether the actions of thirteen states in 2004 in favor of constitutional amendments banning same-sex marriage constituted a trend, Mayor West answered:

I don't doubt that they are. For two reasons: Conservatives know how to organize, and conservatives fight like hell. Some liberals know how to organize, but liberals never fight for anything.

Let's oversimplify this down to two sides of pro and con, ignoring that many people are in a gray area here. If the "no" side is well organized and doesn't back down, and if the "yes" side is poorly organized and backs down in deference to people who agree with the other side, of course you'll have the "no" side winning and the "yes" side losing.

I've never been a Democrat. I was independent for years and have been Green for six. But I still get disappointed when I see these great opportunities for the Democratic Party to take a stand, and time and again, see them collapse and fail. Of course it's going to be a lopsided fight against Republicans.

In the past few decades, well-funded groups like the Christian Coalition took over the county and state apparatuses of the Republican Party, particularly in the South. They were brilliant grass-roots organizers with a bottom line, a line in the sand that you're punished for crossing. They say, "If you're in favor of this issue, we take you down." The fear from that threat is what politics is all about. You need that threat, or people don't know how to act. And that's the kind of political organization that's opposed to marriage equality.

But organizations in favor of marriage equality, like the Human Rights Campaign and Freedom to Marry, do the exact opposite. No matter how many times the Democratic candidate slaps them in the face, they come back and put money and resources in his campaign. So of course John Kerry isn't going to listen to their issues. Rather, he's got to listen to people who've drawn lines in the sand.

If I know that you're going to vote for me anyway, I can ignore you. It's simple politics. When you have organizations dedicated to marriage equality endorse a presidential candidate who is opposed to marriage equality, then of course you'll have ballot initiatives [against same-sex marriage] that are overwhelmingly supported.

So unless those in favor of marriage equality learn how to become effective organizers with a bottom line that they don't allow people to cross, you'll see a continuation of such ballot initiatives. The only way to fight back is to have the right so scared of the left's backlash when the right takes action that they're paralyzed with fear.

The people who oppose marriage equality understand how power works. Most liberals don't.

The Business of Same-Sex Marriage

As introduced in the California chapter, the struggle for same-sex marriage also impacts business. That component of the debate was manifested a month after the New Paltz marriages, when Manhattan's Jacob K. Javits Convention Center hosted a Same-Sex Wedding Expo within the larger annual Gay, Lesbian, Bisexual, and Transgender Expo, in its eleventh year. More than 21,000 people attended the two-day event. Several agents of the merchants and interest groups renting the twenty-five to thirty booths in the Expo's marriage section talked about their businesses.

Terry Shaw represented Imagine Weddings and Events International.

Q: What's the nature of your business?
A: We are planners for weddings around the world. We help couples from the very beginning right up through the end to when they're newly married.

Q: How long have you been doing this?

A: Since January 2000.

Q: Have you seen your business increase recently?

A: Yes. Our business in general has increased. We did 5,000 weddings last year. We do business with most of the major cruise lines. With all the recent attention to same-sex marriages, that business is increasing as well. There's a lot of interest in that.

Q: Of the 5,000 weddings last year, how many of those were same-sex?

A: Probably only about 5 percent. Unfortunately.

Q: Do you see same-sex marriages becoming a more substantial portion of your business?

A: Absolutely.

Q: What percentage do you expect it might become?

A: I would hope 50 percent. [He smiles.]

Q: Are there more same-sex couples contacting your business from particular parts of the country, say, like Massachusetts?

A: No. That's interesting. There are those people who are concerned about the legalities of the ceremony. And there are other people who really don't care. They would like to have a ceremony, no matter what you call it – whether it's a wedding, a commitment ceremony, a civil union, or whatever – in a place where they want it to be, whether St. Thomas, Bali, or Rio de Janeiro.

Troy McDevitt is the sole proprietor of the McDevitt Studio.

Q: What's the nature of your business?

A: I make custom wedding cake toppers that are made to look like the bride and groom. A couple provides me with photos of themselves, and then I use those pictures to sculpt cake toppers that look like them.

Q: How long have you been in business?

A: Since January 2004.

Q: What prompted you to start?

A: I've been a graphic designer for twelve years and always played with sculpting for fun on the side. Because of that, my wife wanted me to do the cake topper for our wedding four years ago. So once I did that, she's been after me to do this business ever since.

Q: Has your business prospered?

A: It's been amazing. It's been phenomenal! You'd think that I just invented, like, bread or sex. [He laughs.] We never anticipated this kind of response.

Q: Can you give numbers?

A: Since January, I've only been to four conventions, and this is my first gay convention. So most of my response so far has been from straight couples. But the response at this convention has been just as phenomenal as at those. I tell people that I have only a five-spot availability per month. So as five orders come in per month, that's all I can do. So I tell them to put their orders in as soon as possible to reserve their place down the road.

Q: Have there been any interesting or humorous requests for cake toppers from same-sex couples?

A: Surprisingly, not really. The most odd one – and it's not really odd at all – is that a couple wanted a likeness of their pet added to their topper. But nothing kinky or pushing the envelope. I get really excited about the ones that are out of the ordinary. As you see here [pointing to his booth's display of cake toppers], besides the straight couples, I've got gay couples – two men, two women – and an interracial couple. What I want to do is, like, a pregnant-bride one – a real variety of them, especially showing anything that's, quote, taboo. So I hope I get something like an S&M cake topper order here. I'd love that. It would be so much fun.

Michael S. Goldstein is a lawyer who specializes in adoption and family law in Rye Brook, New York.

Q: How long have you been practicing this kind of law?

A: Twenty-two years.

Q: What's your purpose at this Expo today?

A: To educate same-sex couples and singles that they can adopt children.

Q: Have you seen an increase in interest in that recently?

A: Yes, with all the publicity on same-sex marriage and same-sex adoption, we've seen a tremendous increase.

Q: Can you give any figures?

A: In our practice, where we do about a hundred adoptions every year, maybe 2 percent of our business was from same-sex couples six or seven years ago. Now it's closer to 10 percent. It's gone up tremendously.

Q: Do you perform other family legal services for same-sex couples?

A: We do adoption-related services, such as second-parent adoptions. We also do re-adoptions, where one of the partners in a same-sex couple will go overseas, adopt, and return to this country. Then he or she re-adopts the child under state law here, with his or her partner usually also adopting as a second parent.

Public Education

A week after the wedding expo, the Stonewall Democratic Club of Rockland County and the Empire State Pride Agenda co-sponsored a "Town Meeting on Marriage and LGBT Families" at the Nanuet Public Library, about thirty miles north of New York City. Ross Levi, the Pride Agenda's Director of Public Policy and Governmental Affairs, moderated, pointing out that this was the fifth of ten statewide town meetings planned by the Pride Agenda. About 150 people attended.

Levi began by distinguishing between civil marriage and religious marriage, and then asked the audience what words came to mind when they heard "marriage." Someone called out "love," and another shouted "commitment." Soon there was a flood: "loyalty," "future," "fidelity," "family," "legality," "children," "taxes," "benefits," "wedding," "divorce," "responsibility," "acceptance," "toasters," and "registries."

Levi noted that there are more than 1,800 legal rights and responsibilities arising from marriage: the General Accounting Office has identified 1,138 federal ones, and the Pride Agenda more than 700 state-created ones. On the federal side are Social Security survivor benefits, immigration rights, the marriage tax bonus, veterans' survivor benefits, and pension rights. Levi emphasized that not one of these rights can be achieved except through the institution of marriage, because that's how federal law confers them. Marriage in New York State supplies rights with regard to hospital visitation and decision making, inheritance, the transfer of property assets, burial decisions, divorce, and the presumption of parenthood. Levi said that between 6 and 10 million children are being raised by lesbian and gay parents across the United States. In the last U.S. Census, there were 46,000 households in New York State that self-identified as same-sex households, with at least one in every county of the state. Twenty-five percent of those households are raising children.

To illustrate these issues, local families provided testimonials at the town meeting. Jason and Mark said they'd been together almost seven years.

Mark: We don't face discrimination on a daily basis. We've been lucky. We've bought furniture and cars and real estate together, and our being a couple never once became an issue.

The first time it really happened was when we sought to become foster parents. We weren't able officially to foster children together because we're not married. The Rockland County Department of Social Services certified both of us individually as foster parents, but when the time came to place Talia with us, she became only Jason's. In all the court papers having Jason's name, mine was no where to be found. When they placed the second child with us, again, my name was no where there, simply because we're not married.

We just recently adopted. Or I actually should say, Jason just recently adopted. Talia is now officially his. But again, we have to apply for a second-parent adoption because New York State won't allow us to do it together because we're two men. Even though she's lived with us for two years, and she's just as equally my child, she's legally only Jason's at this point.

Jason: In addition to that, Mark's not covered under any of my benefits. I work for a school and have a pension and really good medical benefits. But they don't recognize Mark as someone I can cover under my benefits because we're not married. So I'm paying for a family, because I do have a child right now, but I can't include Mark. He has to pay for his own policy.

Furthermore, I have to worry about the pension and Social Security, because if something happens to me, Mark is only covered until Talia is eighteen. So we have to purchase additional life insurance policies and draw up more legal documents just to protect him if, God forbid, something happens to me, or vice versa.

That's the sort of stuff we face as a family that's trying to get the same rights as any married couple in the country. There's a lot more thought and expense that have to go into it. It's just not the given for us that it is for so many other people.

Mark added, "It's really not fair," and then read aloud a letter to the editor published recently in a local newspaper.

"Children Face New Bias. If a lesbian couple marrying somehow arrange to 'have' children, the children will be deprived of a father's love. Similarly, if a homosexual male couple marrying somehow arrange to 'have' children, the children will be deprived of a mother's love. This discrimination against children, individually and as a class, is already occurring when states allow gay couples to adopt. Gay marriage and adoption are the most aggressive way to oppose gender diversity. The effect of this upon society will be horrific and will give those who oppose American democracy a new weapon in their propaganda arsenal. Please contact your state and national legislators. A constitutional amendment may be what is necessary to save children from this form of child abuse. But there can be little doubt that when hearings begin, some children raised by homosexual couples will testify about how 'normal' their childhoods are. Pro-homosexual psychologists can be counted on as well."

At the town meeting Mark next read a rebuttal letter written by his father, who was in the back of the room.

"When I first read this letter to the editor, I became very angry. Then I felt very sad, not for the children that the writer alleges are abused because of homosexual parents, but for the writer himself. I have a son who is thirty-two years old and gay. His torturous adolescence taught me that homosexuality is not a choice but rather who you are, probably at birth. His incredible strength and the unconditional love of his entire family have helped him to become the remarkable man that he is today. Mark and Jason, his life partner of six years, have just recently adopted their daughter –"

Shouts of "Daddy, Daddy!" came from the back of the room. "And that's her," Mark added. "Daddy, Daddy!" continued from the back, as the audience broke into laughter. Mark continued his father's letter:

"She arrived as a very fragile six-week-old premature infant. Talia's natural mother has extreme emotional problems and would have put Talia's life in jeopardy. But instead, Talia today is a healthy, self-confident, very precocious two-year-old, full of love and hope. With the support of extended family –"

Talia romped to the front of the room, bounded into Jason's arms, kissed both of her fathers, and totally stole the show. Mark persevered with his father's letter.

"– with the support of extended family that includes great-great-grandparents and her own incredible parents, Talia will reach her full potential. I doubt that there is any hope for the letter writer. His prejudice appears to have consumed him. As for me, I just thank God every day for the precious gift He has given me."

The next couple to speak at the town meeting were Ileana and Chris.

Ileana: We met about eight years ago in college. We relocated to Rockland, and after seven years together, decided to get married. We went to an Episcopal priest, who agreed to do our ceremony at Grace Episcopal. We hired a lawyer, got a legal name change, wills, health care proxies, and powers of attorney. And when refinancing, we put both names on the mortgage.

Yet we still find that a church marriage doesn't count for much in our lives. Even though our families have come a long way and now accept us in the family, we really don't get the same respect or acknowledgment as, say, Chris's brother and his wife do.

Chris: I'm more practical, thinking a lot about money. We paid for a big wedding. We also had to pay for lawyers that, if we were straight, we wouldn't have had to worry about at all. Yet thank God for our lawyers, because they put us on layaway [laughter]. So we were able to make monthly payments to afford the legal expense. And as women who don't make as much money as men, we have to think more about how to build a future.

Fortunately, I'm very open [as a lesbian] at my job, which is great. But the underlying fact of our not being legally married creates problems at work. When Ileana's father passed away, for example, I had to take time off from my job to visit her family. My boss is familiar with the legal battles facing gay people. Yet he still questioned how I could get bereavement benefits when we're not really married. So he and I had to sit down and discuss how the employment handbook's policies affect our relationship.

When traveling for my job, I make sure to tell all fifteen of my co-workers there, "I love Ileana. I really do. In case I die, just remember that everything goes to her." Although my family has come around quite a bit, they could still contest my will. So every time I travel, I do this round-about, and everyone in the office says, "Yes, we *know* that you love her" [more laughter]. And I respond, "Yeah, but please understand that, if worse comes to worst, I want you to go to court and tell the story of our relationship."

Occasionally, I think about moving to different places. My favorite is Florida, because it's warm. But I also fear what that would mean to our family. If one of us had a child, would the other be able to adopt him or her? New York is a progressive state, and we're probably going to have to stay here until our family evolves. So every time I think, "Oh, it's time to move," we have to talk about the legal issues surrounding our family and future.

Chip was the next speaker.

I am here carrying my partner in my heart and in a picture frame. [He displayed a framed photograph.] Because he himself cannot be here. Almost two years ago, he lost his job in the financial field in New York. What that meant to us was that he would have to leave the country, because losing his job also meant losing his work visa for the United States.

For almost two years, we've been paying extremely high phone bills and airfare to be together. The Atlantic Ocean is a hefty commute, and while the place I often now travel to is Paris – and everyone says, "Oh, you're so lucky: Paris!" – I feel awful that I have no choice but to commute to France to see the person I love.

How ironic this is for me, because the American Psychological Association hires me to fly to conferences to talk about LGBT inclusion in school policies and in mental health trainings. I was also part of the process of creating same-sex inclusive domestic partner benefits in my school district here in Rockland. But I still can't participate in the very benefits I helped develop.

This touches me every day. A lot of the kids I see in my practice and in school I'm helping through divorce and remarriage in their own families. And I'm reminded daily that there's no room for my relationship in this country right now.

SEVEN

Conclusion

THE PRIOR CHAPTERS' NARRATIVES from California, Massachusetts, New Mexico, New York, and Oregon offer in-depth perspectives on America's struggle for same-sex marriage. Yet those stories are state-specific, relying in large measure on local events. This chapter expands the focus of the investigation and synthesizes larger lessons from the politics surrounding lesbian and gay couples' search for civil marriage in the United States.

The book's goal, however, is not to provide comprehensive pro and con arguments on every aspect of the debate over same-sex marriage. Other works attempt that objective (e.g., Sullivan 2004; Wolfson 2004). Rather, this volume uses the reports of the people who participated in the momentous same-sex marriage events of 2003 and 2004 as building blocks for a larger edifice of understanding of what they reveal about how citizens, interest groups, and government interact to produce policy in America.

In similar fashion, this chapter proceeds from topics specific to the controversy over same-sex marriage to more general considerations about the roles of government and its institutions.

Procreation and Child Rearing

The 2000 Census reveals that 34 percent of lesbian couples and 22 percent of gay male couples have at least one child under the age of eighteen living in their home, compared with 46 percent of married opposite-sex couples having minor children at home (Cahill 2004: 45–46). That translates into at least 180,000 same-sex couples raising children in the United States in 2000 (Wolfson 2004: 87).

These children arrive in the households of gay and lesbian couples through multiple routes. Some are adopted. Some are there through foster-care placement. Some are the biological offspring from prior relationships with opposite-sex partners. Some result from artificial insemination via sperm donation. Some are the product of surrogate parentage.

Yet none of the children is the biological creation of the same-sex couples themselves. This fact of "basic biology" (Wolfson 2004: 75) forms a significant part of opponents' critique of same-sex marriage. Indeed, same-sex couples' biological inability to procreate permeates the American political debate over civil marriage for lesbians and gay men. Tim Nashif of the Oregon Family Council offered one version of the criticism.

> We believe that the strength of the family – its nucleus – is one man and one woman. And we believe that that's in the best interests of children.
>
> We also believe, however, that other family units need to be supported. Whether that's two women living together who have children in the home, or the reality of single parenthood, or grandparents taking care of grandchildren. They all need to be supported.
>
> But we believe that we need to encourage the family unit – the DNA of society – which is one man and one woman.
>
> The state has a very strong interest in the procreation of children. And the only way that children can be procreated is with one man and one woman. That's the natural way of things. You can call that a moral issue. You can call that a spiritual issue. You can call that a religious issue. I think it crosses all of those lines. And that's why you can get many people to say, "Hey, I don't see how it can be any other way."

Ronald Crews of the Massachusetts Family Institute elaborated on the theme. After a series of prepared questions, I finished all of my meetings with the people interviewed for this study with a general query, asking whether there was anything more about the issue of same-sex marriage that they'd like to add. The overwhelming number had nothing more to say. Crews, a pastor of the Evangelical

Presbyterian Church, had the longest response of anyone to my concluding inquiry:

There is something I want to raise. As I've spoken on this subject [of same-sex marriage], primarily in churches, I've come to a conclusion that many Americans don't understand why some people, particularly evangelical Christians and conservative Catholics, are so concerned about this issue. What is the driving force that makes this so important for us? I want to give some observations that I don't think are known widely out there. They're not new to me, I'm sure. Yet I haven't seen them in print. I'm kind of reluctant to go into this, but I really feel that it needs to be said.

For people of faith, the institution of marriage is not man-made. Those of us who believe in inspirational scripture and have what I call a high view of scripture see that the concept of marriage comes to us from the dawn of creation, even before the Fall.

God created us male and female. He didn't have to create us heterosexual, but He did. And when scripture says that, "I'll make a helper who fits him," the connotation refers to the way our sexual organs are actually made, in the anatomical sense of a "helper who fits him." The Creator speaks the words that a man is joined to his wife and the two become one, and that becomes the biblical understanding of marriage.

And that verse is repeated four times in scripture – there in Genesis, twice by Jesus, quoting that verse in the Gospels, and then once by Paul. And when Paul quotes it in Ephesians five, he gives an additional layer of importance to the institution of marriage, because he says that marriage is a picture of the relationship between Christ and his bride – Christ and the church. And Heaven itself is referred to as the marriage or wedding feast.

So for people of faith, the concept of marriage has deep meaning. We see it in the same way that there is natural law. If you go against natural law, there are consequences. The way I share it when I'm preaching on the subject is that, even if judges decide they don't like the definition of gravity and write a new definition for gravity, if I drop something, it's still going to fall. You cannot rewrite a definition of a word without the word itself being changed or challenged. But the reality is that gravity is still gravity.

In the same way, even though they can write a new definition for marriage, I say that marriage is a part of the moral law, that it was spoken into our very creation. It's in the fiber of His creation. Just as gravity was spoken into the fiber of our natural order, marriage is a part of our moral order. There are consequences when that moral order is violated.

And that's why this is a significant issue for people of faith. It goes right to the core of our understanding of scripture, of what's good, of what's right, and what's best.

Some might say that that's fine for the church, that the church can have its own definition of marriage. But states have been involved in setting policy for the institution of marriage from our country's founding. That goes way back in our history. Legislators have put parameters around the institution of marriage for many years.

In that regard, I use the example that when state legislators said first cousins can't marry first cousins, that didn't make those legislators "cousin-phobes." They just said we're going to set some protections around the institution. So it's a legitimate enterprise for legislators.

Furthermore, it's the duty of legislators, I believe, to set standards for what is the highest, what is the good, what is the ideal. Marriage is an institution that's worked very well in terms of producing and raising children. And I believe, based on the social science evidence that I've read, that children do best when they have a biological mom and dad. Not every child has that opportunity, but that's the ideal setting.

What [the *Goodridge*] court did just overlooked mountains of social science evidence, historical precedent, and the right of legislators to legislate. Instead, by fiat, the court created a social experiment that we won't know the impact of for several generations down the road. What will this do to children who are taught that either men or women aren't necessary? What they've done is create – not homosexual marriage – but fatherless unions and motherless unions. And what will that say to future generations?

The Massachusetts Supreme Judicial Court's majority opinion in *Goodridge* provided a cogent response to the basic biology argument as a prohibition of civil marriage for same-sex couples.

The judge in the [lower court in this case] endorsed the ... rationale ... that "the state's interest in regulating marriage is based on the traditional concept that marriage's primary purpose is procreation." This is incorrect. Our laws of civil marriage do not privilege procreative heterosexual intercourse between married people above every other form of adult intimacy and every other means of creating a family. [The matrimonial law] contains no requirement that the applicants for a marriage license attest to their ability or intention to conceive children by coitus. Fertility is not a condition of marriage, nor is it grounds for divorce. People who have never consummated their marriage, and never plan to, may be and stay married. ... People who cannot stir from their deathbed may marry. ... While it is certainly true that many, perhaps most, married couples have children together (assisted or unassisted), it is the exclusive and permanent commitment of the marriage partners to one another, not the begetting of children, that is the sine qua non of civil marriage.

Moreover, [Massachusetts] affirmatively facilitates bringing children into a family regardless of whether the intended parent is married or unmarried, whether the child is adopted or born into a family, whether assistive technology was used to conceive the child, and whether the parent or her partner is heterosexual, homosexual, or bisexual. If procreation were a necessary component of civil marriage, our statutes would draw a tighter circle around the permissible bounds of nonmarital child bearing and the creation of families by noncoital means. The attempt to isolate procreation as "the source of a fundamental right to marry" . . . overlooks the integrated way in which courts have examined the complex and overlapping realms of personal autonomy, marriage, family life, and child rearing. [American] jurisprudence recognizes that, in these nuanced and fundamentally private areas of life, such a narrow focus is inappropriate. (798 N.E.2d at 961–62)

Other responses to the basic biology and related arguments are available in Sullivan (2004) and Wolfson (2004).

Are Civil Unions/Domestic Partnerships/Reciprocal Benefits Adequate?

The legislatures of California, Connecticut, and Vermont have passed comprehensive systems, called civil unions or domestic partnerships, that provide legal recognition for the relationship rights of lesbian and gay couples. Hawaii and New Jersey provide programs with limited benefits. Additional state legislatures are considering similar plans, but as of 2005, no other such bill passed.

As a result of these developments, a second major argument that opponents of civil marriage for same-sex couples make is that other legal arrangements are available to gay and lesbian couples that effectively grant them everything they need that marriage might bring.

Even President George W. Bush, who publicly endorsed the Federal Marriage Amendment in February 2004, told an interviewer on ABC's *Good Morning America* broadcast of October 26, 2004:

> I don't think we should deny people rights to a civil union, a legal arrangement, if that's what a state chooses to do. ...
>
> I view the definition of marriage different from legal arrangements that enable people to have rights. And I strongly believe that marriage ought to be defined as between a union between a man and a woman.
>
> Now, having said that, states ought to be able to have the right to pass laws that enable people to be able to have rights like others.

Tim Nashif of the Oregon Family Council focused on this prominent theme of the marriage debate.

> I have lots of people working for me. I don't know if they're gay or not. I don't ask them. And I don't like the fact that somebody has to declare their sexual orientation.
>
> So all of a sudden in 2000, if you want civil unions the way that Vermont laid them out, you have to declare you're gay, because Vermont wanted to make sure they weren't available to heterosexuals.
>
> I don't like the idea of declaring sexual orientation. Plus the fact that, no matter what you do, no matter how you go, you're still exclusionary. Once you stretch those benefits to one community or group, well, there'll be somebody else coming along who also wants them but is left out.

Hawaii handled it a totally different way, with reciprocal benefits. That means that anybody who does not qualify for marriage has access to this group of benefits, with no language about sexual orientation, and nothing pointing at specific groups of people.

It covers any two people who want to sign an agreement that says, "We care for one another; we want to help one another; we do not qualify for marriage; but we'd like to have these benefits." Then, with that agreement, the benefits automatically apply. I think that's a very intelligent way to go.

I've checked with a number of pastors in our circuit here, and they've agreed. They say, "We have people in our churches that would benefit from this." So what are the gay activists going to do now? Are they going to say, "No, wait a minute. We want it to apply just to us. We don't want it to go to other individuals who might have need of these benefits."

There are several responses to Nashif's criticisms of same-sex couples' quest for marriage. The first considers whether the benefits of marriage are indeed already available to lesbian and gay partners.

Clearly, all couples, heterosexual and homosexual, can pay attorneys to prepare wills, durable powers of attorney, health care proxies, hospital visitation authorizations, "living" wills, and other documents that regulate couples' legal and economic relationships. Moreover, many public and private employers provide health insurance and other benefits to their employees' same-sex partners. For example, about half of Fortune 500 companies do, including Ford, General Electric, General Motors, and IBM.

Yet there are goods available to couples for which civil marriage is the exclusive gateway. No matter how well lesbian and gay pairs plan their lives, there's nothing they can do to secure these goods without governmental recognition of their relationship. Indeed, the relationship can be destroyed without the benefit of marriage, as in the circumstance of binational couples, exemplified by Chip's story in the last chapter.

Other important, albeit less severe, consequences flow to same-sex couples without the legal tie of marriage. Recall from the New York chapter how Chris and Ileana were nearly denied bereavement leave by a gay-sympathetic employer. Also consider the economic impact on one of the pairs receiving marriage licenses in Multnomah County in 2004.

Brian and Doug have been together for eleven years. Doug has legal custody of his teenage daughter (from a previous marriage to a woman). Brian's employer provides family health insurance and other benefits to the dependents (including domestic partners and their children) of its employees. Doug and his daughter thus are covered under the policy of Brian's employer. If Doug were Brian's heterosexual spouse, that would be the end of the story.

However, the Internal Revenue Service imputes the fair market value of the health insurance and other benefits given to Doug and his daughter as additional income to Brian. Under the Defense of Marriage Act, the IRS doesn't recognize Doug and his daughter as part of Brian's family, even though they all live together. As a result, Brian pays federal income tax on the imputed value of the benefits to Doug and his daughter. In 2003, that amounted to approximately $9,000 of further taxable income to Brian. Moreover, this additional income to Brian's salary puts him into a higher tax bracket. Thus, every year, Brian and Doug pay thousands of dollars in taxes that married opposite-sex couples don't have to worry about. The same tax penalty befalls every gay and lesbian couple receiving employer-sponsored domestic-partner benefits in the United States.

A more poignant tale comes from Massachusetts, where three sources confirmed the narrative. Arline Isaacson of the Massachusetts Gay and Lesbian Political Caucus provided details.

> This is a story about two elderly lesbians, one a retired schoolteacher, whom I'll call Susan, and the other a retired nurse, whom I'll call Mary. Susan and Mary lived together forever.
>
> When Mary, the nurse, was actively nursing, she focused a lot of her attention and energy on issues around homelessness and senior citizens. As a result of her hard work, a homeless shelter for senior citizens was first established in Massachusetts.
>
> After retirement, Mary fell and injured her hip, a common accident with seniors. Susan, the retired schoolteacher, was afraid that Mary would have to be put into a nursing home, because

Susan, herself frail, might not be able to give Mary the full care she needed.

In Massachusetts – and I believe this is true in other states as well – there's something called the Medicaid Empoverishment Spousal Waiver. That means that if a legally recognized spouse is put into a nursing home and the other spouse can't afford to pay for the treatment because of inadequate resources, the state will pay for it under Medicaid. But the state says, "If we're paying to maintain you in a nursing home, we're taking your assets. But wait a minute. You're a married couple and have lived in a house that you've shared together for many years. We'll let the healthy spouse stay in the house and keep a few thousand dollars of joint assets. Other than that, we're taking everything." That's if you're straight.

If you're a gay or lesbian couple, the spousal waiver doesn't apply. Well, Mary, the retired nurse, owned the home that she and Susan lived in, having bought it decades earlier, before the two women met. Title was in Mary's name only. They never bothered to put Susan's name on the deed. They didn't think they needed to.

So if Mary had to go into a nursing home, the state would come along and say, "We're paying the Medicaid for Mary's nursing home. You know what, Susan? You're not Mary's legal spouse. So we're taking all of Mary's assets, including her house, and you're evicted from it." Susan, the retired schoolteacher, would be left only with a minuscule monthly pension to live on.

Thus, the painful irony was that Susan could end up in the homeless shelter for seniors that Mary had set up.

These are examples of just some of the goods that are available to couples only through the gateway of civil marriage. More comprehensive lists of such benefits are available in Wolfson (2004) and on the Web site of the Human Rights Campaign (www.hrc.org). Yet these limited accounts dispel the notions that civil unions and domestic partnerships are equivalent to civil marriage and that merely fabricated or hypothetical problems motivate same-sex couples' marriage quest.

Kate Kendell of the National Center for Lesbian Rights elaborated on the inadequacies of civil unions, domestic partnerships, and reciprocal benefits.

If I ruled this sphere of human life, I would have a civil union/ domestic partner scheme as part of a social contract for every couple, gay or nongay. Then, if people want to get married, they go to their church. In fact, I would even go a step further and have there be a menu of choices, where some couples would want all the federal and state rights and responsibilities that go along with this civil contract, and some would want everything but X, Y, and Z. I don't think marriage is an answer for every couple and family. It's not a one-size-fits-all solution. So I would have it be more complex and flexible.

But you know what? I'm going to win the lottery tomorrow, too. I'm a realist and know that my fantasy isn't going to happen in this culture. Instead, the optimal way that security and protection are provided to families is through marriage. Even the most muscular domestic partner scheme doesn't do that. For instance, there are the practical lapses, including a complete lack of federal benefits and protections. Some of these are very important, like Social Security survivor benefits, the right to sponsor a partner for immigration purposes in binational relationships, and Medicaid and Medicare programs. Lots of different federal benefits are unavailable to same-sex couples in California and Vermont and Massachusetts.

And there's no portability. When our car rolls over the state line, my partner and I are legal strangers, even though we're registered domestic partners here [in California]. So it's just not the same as a practical matter.

There's also a dignitary issue. If domestic partner schemes are so good and equivalent to marriage, then I'd like to reverse the situation and have all straight people be in domestic partnerships, and we'll be the ones to get married.

Everyone understands that there's a social good recognized in marriage. There's a celebration of marriage that's not the same for couples in domestic partner schemes. Their very creation in fact is a way of appeasing the opponents of same-sex marriage, rather than actually providing full equality and security to lesbian and gay couples.

People who are uncomfortable with gay folk getting married want us to accept domestic partner schemes precisely because they think we're not worthy of marriage. And I just reject that from an emotional and social equivalency standpoint. I'm going to fight against that as long as marriage is the social construct in this country.

Acceptance or Bigotry?

In an earlier quotation, MFI's Ronald Crews stated that legislators' prohibition of marriages between first cousins didn't make them "cousin-phobes." Indeed, American matrimonial law contains several consanguinity proscriptions. Yet the legislators who passed those limitations on the capacity to marry believed that procreation by people closely related to one another by blood produced children with genetic defects (Ottenheimer 1996).

In a similar vein, nonetheless, those who resist civil marriage for same-sex couples disparage the notion that they're hostile to gay people. Again, OFC's Tim Nashif:

> What gay activists really want is for people to approve of their lifestyle or be boxed into an inference of bigotry. Gay activists are trying to force public policy that brings legitimacy to their lifestyle and has people who disagree with them be considered less than good citizens.
>
> This debate isn't about benefits. It's not about the actual institution of marriage. Rather, it's about what they call equality in thinking, where everyone has got to either accept them or be a bigot.
>
> We take exception to that. We don't agree with it. There are people who don't want to discriminate against gays, and I'm one of them. Yet because of different religious or spiritual views, we may not approve of their lifestyle, but do not believe they should be persecuted for it.
>
> We might teach against it. We might speak against it. However, that doesn't mean that people do not have a free choice in this nation to live their lives whatever way they want to live them, free of any kind of discrimination. But that does not also mean that their lifestyle has to be condoned, or that people have to be forced to accept it under penalty of law through hate crimes legislation and all these other things, when no real problem exists in the first place.

And no real problem does exist in the first place. It's a manu-factured problem. If there is a problem that really does exist, then why talk about benefits that, if you were honest with yourself, are already available?

What they really want is recognition. They want affirmation. And they want to force people to accept their lifestyle or be categorized as less than good citizens. That's the way we view it.

NCLR's Kate Kendell responded to this argument when she considered Nashif's comment that he didn't like the idea of people declaring their sexual orientation.

That statement is by someone who walks in the world with tre-mendous heterosexual privilege. No one has to declare their sex-ual orientation in American culture because *everyone* is presumed to be heterosexual. If you do declare that you're not, then you open yourself up, not only to discrimination and recrimination, but to the charge of flaunting. That is, you've said something that no one else *needs* to say, because heterosexuality is assumed.

I think this is true of white folks who are racist. It's also true of white folks who aren't racist but who don't unpack their own privilege.

When people walk through the world with multiple privileges – and he's got a bunch of them: male, white, heterosexual – it's just so arrogant of them to make those kinds of statements. His position betrays complete ignorance about how heterosexual privilege operates and how the declaration of one's sexual orien-tation as lesbian or gay is actually a mark of authenticity and integrity in this culture.

Lesbians and gay men who come out as such don't want to walk through the world with a privilege that they don't deserve. They want to make it clear, "This is who I am," and then accept whatever society's reaction is. No one should want to exercise a privilege that's not theirs.

Just spend some time reflecting on the hubris of a statement condemning declarations of sexual orientation. They come from people who don't like gays and are framed in ways that appeal to the middle-of-the-road folks who haven't made up their mind. "Yeah, it makes me uncomfortable when people say they're gay."

But no one ever says something like, "Bill talked about going to the movie with his wife last night. I was so uncomfortable with that." Such double standards never cease to amaze me, with their complete lack of appreciation of how gay people are forced to operate in an overwhelmingly heterosexist culture.

In light of Kendell's appraisal, two events from my interview of Tim Nashif are pertinent here. First, during a two-hour, wide-ranging discussion, Nashif mentioned his wife to me on two separate occasions. In neither instance did I ask him a question that solicited such a reference. That is, I didn't seek the information he volunteered. Weren't those remarks about his wife declarations of his sexual orientation (i.e., that he, a man, is married to a woman)? By inference, then, Nashif's objection to announcements of sexual orientation appears applicable only to proclamations by lesbians and gay men.

Second, in the last part of the interview, Nashif said to me: "My wife and I don't [do something]. We would never do that. I don't think you and your wife would do that." I never had occasion, before or during our meeting, to identify my sexual orientation to him – although as the second chapter of this book suggests, I don't hesitate to say that I'm gay when such information is relevant. Nonetheless, Nashif did presume that I'm heterosexual.

Kendell offered a more general response to Nashif's critique of gay and lesbian couples' search for marriage.

> It's impossible for me to divorce a statement like that – that could otherwise be seen as rational – from someone whose life's work is about denying equality and fairness to lesbian and gay people. This guy is not like my former brother-in-law, who isn't really comfortable with gay people and probably doesn't agree on marriage. But he's not going to devote a whole lot of time and energy and money to the issue.
>
> But to the point. On the basis of equality and fairness and constitutional principle, government does, or ignores, lots of things, in terms of differences, that people don't agree with. No one has to vote on or approve of me as a lesbian, my relationship, or the desire of lesbian and gay people to get married, in order to

hold the view that government has no business denying legal recognition to lesbian and gay relationships. And if you think you do, then mind your own business.

It's none of anyone's business how the government gives benefits. That's the government's business. And our position is that the government has no right drawing a line and saying certain people are in and other folks are out.

I'm sure that lots of people still can't abide, and experience revulsion at, the idea of interracial marriage, particularly a white woman walking down the street, arm in arm, with a ring on her finger, married to a black man. They don't approve of it at all. But they don't get any say anymore about whether the government should issue a marriage license to that couple. The same thing applies to same-sex pairs.

Polling data are available to bolster Kendell's assertion regarding interracial marriage. For example, when the U.S. Supreme Court decided *Loving v. Virginia* (1967), striking down state interracial-marriage prohibitions, 72 percent of Americans opposed marriage between people of different races, and 48 percent thought it should be a crime (Cahill 2004: 13).

As Ronald Crews of the Massachusetts Family Institute revealed at the beginning of the chapter, much of the resistance to same-sex marriage is based on religious beliefs. Indeed, Crews feared anti-religious backlash in the event that same-sex marriage becomes widespread in the United States.

We may see evidence in this country of what happened in Canada and Sweden. There's a pastor in jail right now [2004] in Sweden because he preached a sermon against homosexuality. A criminal allegation of hate speech was brought against him, and he was sentenced to one month in jail.

There's another pastor, in Canada, who has not been sentenced yet, but who is awaiting court. The charge again is for hate speech, because he put a direct quotation about homosexuality from Leviticus on the bulletin board outside his church. If that becomes a consequence of this behavior, if pastors start going to jail in Massachusetts for sermons about homosexuality, then I think we all are in a nether ball game.

For the purpose of uniform crime reporting in the United States, the Federal Bureau of Investigation defines "hate crime" as "a criminal offense committed against a person or property which is motivated, in whole or in part, by the offender's bias against a race, religion, disability, ethnicity/national origin, or sexual orientation." Thus, in America, hate crimes refer only to behavior that is already criminalized as antisocial, such as murder or assault.

Moreover, the First Amendment protects most forms of pure speech in the United States. Unless ministers incite their parishioners to riot, I don't see how Ronald Crews's fears of criminal prosecution of pastors for speaking out against homosexuality or same-sex marriage are justified. Quotations from Leviticus posted on a bulletin board are unlikely sparks for civil rampage.

Nonetheless, Crews's statements reveal the critical nexus between religious beliefs and opposition to civil marriage for lesbian and gay couples. Note that Crews's examples concern religious leaders' statements about homosexuality, not same-sex marriage. The Canadian and Swedish pastors were concerned as much with single gay men and lesbians as they were with those in pairs. The same is true regarding Crews's reliance on the biblical phrase about a "helper who fits him."

Further evidence of the link between religious beliefs and opposition to same-sex marriage lies in the extensive participation of churches in the Measure 36 campaign reported by Tim Nashif in the Oregon chapter. At least 1,200 of the Beaver State's approximately 3,000 churches collected a minimum of 65,000 signatures on petitions to ban civil marriage for lesbian and gay couples. What is more, in a May 2005 national poll commissioned by the *Boston Globe*, 62 percent of respondents expressing opposition to gay marriage said they were against it for religious or moral reasons (Greenberger 2005).

Writing in the *New York Times*, Russell Shorto, who conducted a lengthy study in Maryland of organized opposition to same-sex marriage, reported his assessment of what motivates the people he described as "anti-gay-marriage crusaders":

> [F]or the anti-gay-marriage activists, homosexuality is something to be fought, not tolerated or respected. I found no one among the people who are leading the anti-gay-marriage cause who said in essence: "I have nothing against homosexuality. I just don't believe gays should be allowed to marry." Rather, their passion comes from their conviction that homosexuality is a sin, is immoral, harms children and spreads disease. Not only that, but they see homosexuality itself as a kind of disease, one that afflicts not only individuals but also society at large and that shares one of the prominent features of a disease: it seeks to spread itself. (Shorto 2005: 37)

My own meetings with the leaders of the anti-same-sex marriage movements in Massachusetts and Oregon – the two states in 2004 with the most rigorous political campaigns involving the issue – confirm this appraisal. In particular, the statements in the book by Crews and Nashif belie avowals of dispassion toward homosexuals, whether single or coupled.

Webster's New World Dictionary defines "bigot" as either "a person who holds blindly and intolerantly to a particular creed, opinion, etc." or "a narrow-minded person." Readers can decide for themselves whether the description fits here.

At minimum, though, much of oppositional belief is based on stereotypes of gay men and lesbians. For example, consider this statement by Tim Nashif quoted above in chapter 5.

> Some gays don't want to get married. They understand each other, that this particular relationship is fine, but it may last for only two or three years, because it's the nature of their relationships. They are not intended for a lifetime. It's not the nature of their culture. I'm not going to say it's not the nature of everyone in their culture. There's a diversity there. But for the most part, if you look at the statistics, it's clear.

As an empiricist, I can't imagine which *reliable* statistics he's referring to. As the Appendix points out, empirically based generalizations about the American lesbian and gay community are exceptionally difficult to make, if only because it's virtually impossible to identify the relevant population accurately.

Nonetheless, I did collect information about the duration of the relationships among the fifty same-sex couples interviewed for this book. As of the dates of the interviews in 2004 and 2005, they had been together, on average, 15.9 years. The shortest relationship was three years; the longest, 33. The average age of the 100 gay men and lesbians in the sample was 47.4 years. The youngest person was 30; the oldest, 78.

Since these fifty pairs were selected as randomly as could be done under the circumstances (again, the process is explained in the Appendix), there's no good reason to believe that the mean 15.9-year relationship duration isn't reasonably representative of the larger population of gay and lesbian couples who married in the United States in 2004.

Thus, generalized statements such as "[gay relationships] last for only two or three years, because ... [t]hey are not intended for a lifetime [and i]t's not the nature of their culture" are grounded more on myth than empiricism.

The Roles of Courts and Legislatures

Another common theme among same-sex marriage opponents focuses on which branch of government should weigh whether to extend civil marriage to same-sex partners, which motif Tim Nashif articulated.

> Legislators, not judges, should be dealing with this issue. Lawmakers have gotta listen to hearings. They've gotta go through the motions. They've gotta look at what's on the books and define it in a way to make it work.
>
> Legislators are sensitively going to listen to hearings and people's response to concerns on both sides. When an activist judge drops a gavel and says, this is the way it should be, he has no clear understanding of the ramifications all the way down the board on

how that choice is going to affect the economy, jobs, and society. He has no idea.

So the judicial system has to be very careful not to preempt the legislative process and responsibility. Likewise with the executive branch. That's why executives have full veto power. But they don't have veto power over the judiciary, which is a concern.

Furthermore, I can find just as many judges who don't believe that marriage should be extended to same-sex couples as I can judges who think that it should be. So judges don't agree on the issue. If that's the way society goes, then we've got chaos.

We have a much more active judiciary than we had fifty years ago, seventy-five years ago, or a hundred years ago. It's a major concern, and that's why it's spoken about so often. People worry about whether judges are strict constructionists or whether they believe that the Constitution is an evolving document that should change however they see fit to transform it.

Kate Kendell supplied a rejoinder to this analysis.

Go back to your Political Science 101 class and pay attention this time. We have a system in this country that understands that sometimes there are prejudices that inflame the popular consciousness in illegitimate ways. Folks then aren't feeling or acting rationally. They don't approach issues presented to them in a manner that is measured and fair.

So we have the judiciary and the legislature as checks on that bias. And sometimes the judiciary checks the legislature, because lawmakers can often be caught up in the same prejudice.

Until the issue of same-sex marriage came to prominence in this country, no one seriously suggested that we put civil rights up to a popular vote.

Race provides an interesting analogy here. If Americans were allowed to determine, on a state-by-state basis, whether racial identity should be accorded full constitutional protection, I dare say that there are certainly some counties and perhaps some states in this country that would reinstate portions of Jim Crow.

Two relevant ballot measures – one in South Carolina in 1998, the other in Alabama in 2000 – prove the point. Both states had provisions in their constitutions prohibiting interracial marriage, even though the Supreme Court determined *in 1967* that such laws violate the federal Constitution. Although majorities repealed the bans, a whopping 40 percent of voters in both Alabama and South Carolina wanted to keep the racist language in their state charters.

So until recently, America hasn't put civil rights up to popular votes, because we recognize that sometimes we're not our better selves. Sometimes our better angels are not what come to the fore. We have legislators act first. But if they're caught up in the same momentary hostility, then the judiciary is the guarantor of more calm and reasoned judgment.

Courts look at the law and say, "We understand you're not comfortable with this. This result may not be how you would vote if given the chance. But we have a system of laws in this country. Our conclusion is what the Constitution demands, and its standards should be applied fairly and rationally. These people should not be excluded from its protections."

I wouldn't want the Ku Klux Klan to march on City Hall. But guess what? They have the right to do so, regardless of majority opinion. Indeed, there are many activities that aren't politically popular, that the majority in this country wouldn't vote in favor of tomorrow, but that nonetheless *are* protected by our Constitution.

It's fascinating to me how much play and traction this whole "activist judge" rhetoric gets. Certainly the President parlays the phrase into great political points for himself. But it's really a dangerous concept when applied to marginalized communities in this country. Critics of marriage equality forget our system's structure and that we have a Bill of Rights.

Sherri Sokeland Kaiser, a deputy attorney for the City and County of San Francisco, summarized the point the following way.

Courts are an antidemocratic branch. They have a function different from making decisions by popular majority will. Yet that doesn't mean they're an activist branch. Rather, judges make decisions based on principles set forth in the Constitution or in popularly enacted laws.

When courts enforce constitutional principles, quite often they do so on behalf of minorities that can't command popular support, but that nonetheless have very legitimate and ringing claims to the same rights everyone else has in the Constitution. And I think same-sex marriage is exactly that situation.

Judicial Efficacy

I return now to a political science theme introduced in chapter 2: the debate over whether courts can effect significant social change in the United States or whether they are just deceptively hollow hopes that sap social reformers' resources and spirit. The Massachusetts Supreme Judicial Court's decisions in *Goodridge* and *Opinions* (collectively referred to as "*Goodridge*") are the crucible for judicial impact here, while same-sex marriage is the crusade.

I first consider *Goodridge*'s negative effects (i.e., those impeding the social-movement goal of civil marriage for same-sex couples) and then its positive outcomes. The book's data (see the Appendix) from political elites, both officials and interest groups, provide a top-down perspective on *Goodridge*. Leading actors in relevant states offer opinions about the consequence of the SJC's decisions in their jurisdictions and the nation. In contrast, the rulings' consumers (Canon 1998), the married same-sex couples, supply a grass-roots, bottom-up view of judicial impact.

Backlash

The clearest indicator of public recoil to *Goodridge* is the thirteen states in 2004 that adopted constitutional amendments banning same-sex marriage. The Oregon chapter reveals unequivocally that the Massachusetts case was the primary impetus in the Beaver State for Measure 36. Tim Nashif, whose organization authored Measure 36, explained the group's motivation.

> Massachusetts was on the verge of legalizing same-sex marriage. ... So the question came up, if Massachusetts legalizes same-sex marriage, how do we deal with the fact that [lesbian and gay] Oregonians may be able to go to Massachusetts, get married, come back to Oregon, and then we have a situation in Oregon

where there's this debate about whether these marriages should be recognized? ...

[All of our discussions were] in the context of Massachusetts. [They were] never in the context of Oregon because ... no one had ever tried to promote same-sex marriage in Oregon before. ... So it would have to become a judicial activist situation, which was a concern for us because of what happened in Massachusetts. No one had even thought of that as a big enough concern until what took place in Massachusetts.

Moreover, as indicated in chapter 5, the Oregon Family Council submitted the citizen initiative to the Oregon Secretary of State's office the week before the Multnomah County commissioners' public announcement of their decision to grant marriage licenses to same-sex partners.

It's reasonable to assume that *Goodridge* also motivated activists like Tim Nashif in Arkansas, Georgia, Kentucky, Louisiana, Michigan, Mississippi, Missouri, Montana, North Dakota, Ohio, Oklahoma, and Utah to amend their constitutions in 2004 to prohibit same-sex marriage. No gay or lesbian weddings occurred in those states under the ostensible color of law to prompt local backlash, as happened elsewhere that year.

Kate Kendell's rejoinder to this list was, "These aren't states that were going to promote marriage equality anytime soon anyway." Empirical evidence bolsters this assessment. As of 2005, every American state (California, Connecticut, Hawaii, Massachusetts, New Jersey, and Vermont) that recognized consequential relationship rights among lesbian and gay couples had prior statewide prohibitions of sexual-orientation discrimination in the workplace. Indeed, in every instance, the legislative inclusion of sexual orientation within civil rights statutes proscribing job discrimination preceded, by at least six years, states' adoption of civil unions, domestic partnerships, or other relationship schemes for same-sex couples. Hawaii, for instance, protected gay and lesbian workers from sexual-orientation discrimination starting in 1991. Six years later, the Aloha State legislature passed its reciprocal benefits law. In Vermont, the temporal gap from job protection to civil unions was eight years. In those states where courts didn't prod legislatures to act on relationship rights, the delays were even longer – eleven years in California, fourteen in Connecticut.

None of the thirteen states banning same-sex marriage in 2004 had statewide sexual-orientation discrimination prohibitions in place. Thus, there's no empirical reason to believe that they would have acted favorably to same-sex partners in the near future *but for the Massachusetts court decisions.* This component of the *Goodridge* backlash, therefore, took no state-conferred rights, extant or imminent, away from lesbian and gay couples in Arkansas, Georgia, Kentucky, Louisiana, Michigan, Mississippi, Missouri, Montana, North Dakota, Ohio, Oklahoma, Oregon, and Utah.

As chapter 5 notes, though, nine of the thirteen state constitutional amendments included language proscribing civil-union and domestic-partnership arrangements. These provisions did adversely affect some gay and lesbian pairs.

[Proposal 2, passed by 59 percent of Michigan voters,] has already had a negative impact on the availability of domestic partnership benefits for public employees in Michigan. Shortly before the November 2004 election, the state reached a tentative agreement with five unions that would have provided domestic partnership benefits for represented employees. The ratification of this agreement was postponed, however, because the governor and other state and union officials were reportedly concerned that offering domestic partnership benefits to public employees could potentially violate Proposal 2. These officials claimed that they wanted definitive guidance from the judiciary before providing domestic partnership benefits to public employees once the constitutional amendment was enacted. (Staszewski 2005)

The Wolverine State charter amendment clearly engendered tangible losses for some same-sex couples.

The Michigan experience, however, wasn't a common one. In fact, it appeared to be the exception to a general rule of non-impact for the broadly worded constitutional amendments in the nine states. For instance, more than a year after 62 percent of Ohio voters approved a comprehensive nonmarital-relationship recognition ban, domestic partnership benefits continued for the same-sex partners of many public employees in the Buckeye State. Equally important, few, if any, governmental entities in the other seven states offered benefits to nonmarried couples prior to November 2004. Informed sources confirmed this circumstance in Arkansas, Kentucky, and Utah, and I suspect the same was true in Louisiana, Mississippi, North Dakota, and Oklahoma. Hence, the 2004 voter initiatives had relatively little practical effect.

The second component of the *Goodridge* backlash is the Federal Marriage Amendment. Some gay-marriage adversaries sought thereby to preclude all governmental action favorable to same-sex partners. Recall that President George W. Bush endorsed the FMA, the ratification of which would have the practical effect of fore-closing all federal and state judicial and legislative decisions to include lesbian and gay couples in the marriage institution.

Yet history counsels that the FMA is unlikely ever to receive congressional approval. In March 2004, at the height of media attention to gay and lesbian marriages in New Paltz, Portland, San Francisco, and Sandoval County, the *New York Times* reported that 59 percent of Americans then favored a constitutional amendment allowing marriage only between a man and a woman. Fourteen months later, in May 2005, the Gallup Organization announced that the number of Americans preferring a constitutional amendment dropped to 53 percent. Moreover, according to the 2004 *New York Times*/CBS News poll, just 38 percent thought such an amendment was important enough to change the Constitution.

Those numbers do not a constitutional amendment make. In 1989, the U.S. Supreme Court, relying on the First Amendment's protection of free speech, struck down a Texas law that criminalized burning the American flag. In June 1990, the Court invalidated a similar federal statute. That same month, a Gallup poll reported that 66 percent of Americans favored a constitutional amendment prohibiting flag burning. Nonetheless, Congress passed no such amendment.

A comparable experience occurred with school prayer. After the Supreme Court in the 1960s restricted prayer in public schools, public opinion polls consistently revealed that at least 60 percent of Americans favored amending the Constitution to permit prayer in public schools. But no such amendment made it through Congress.

Additional results from the 2004 *New York Times*/CBS poll are even more toxic to the FMA than this history. Then, 22 percent of Americans backed gay marriage outright, while another 33 percent supported permitting gay couples to form civil unions. In short, a clear majority believed that lesbian and gay couples should have the same legal rights as heterosexual partners.

The final component of the *Goodridge* backlash is the perceived boost the debate over same-sex marriage gave to President Bush's reelection in 2004, as Senator Feinstein mentioned in the California chapter. I report here on the conclusions of political scientists who investigated the issue empirically.

Using both individual and state-level data in a statistical analysis of the impact of same-sex marriage on the 2004 presidential election, Gregory Lewis concluded:

> Same-sex marriage mattered in the 2004 election, less than some issues but more than most. The 2004 election largely replayed an election where gay rights, especially same-sex marriage, played little role. Survey data indicate that the war in Iraq, the economy, and terrorism all had larger impacts on vote choices. (Lewis 2005: 197)

Relying on post-election survey data, another analysis reached a similar conclusion.

> [Most] important to vote choice in the 2004 [presidential] election [were] party identification, ideology, attitudes toward the Iraq war, terrorism, and the economy. Among the most decisive groups – Independents and respondents in battleground states – gay marriage and abortion had no impact on individual vote choice once other factors were controlled. Only in the South did the values issue of gay marriage have an independent effect on

vote choice; yet few ever doubted the strength of the GOP, nor Bush's electoral lead, in the South. ... [T]he moral values issues of gay marriage and abortion matter[ed] most where the campaign mattered least. (Hillygus and Shields 2005: 207)

A third study on the effect of same-sex marriage in the 2004 presidential election found the following.

[W]hile gay marriage was not necessarily the most important factor overall and did not matter equally for every voter, it did matter to white evangelical Christians and Catholics. Specifically, evangelicals and Catholics were more likely to turn out to vote in states with a gay marriage ban on the ballot. At the same time, secular Republicans swung their support away from Bush in these states. States with gay marriage ballot propositions, which included the linchpin of Ohio, afforded Republicans the opportunity to raise gay marriage as an issue with an important subset of their base, which helped Bush. At the same time, however, these efforts also alienated secularly-oriented Republican identifiers, harming Bush. On balance, it appears to have done Bush more good than harm. (Campbell and Monson 2005)

See also Klein (2005) and Sherrill (2005).

Thus, the empirically verifiable repercussions of *Goodridge* appear to be relatively modest. In fact, at least one gay-marriage supporter, Sherri Sokeland Kaiser, the San Francisco deputy city attorney, found consolation in the public recoil to civil marriage for gay and lesbian couples.

What we're seeing now with regard to same-sex marriage is no different from other civil rights struggles in our nation's history. In many ways, the similarity is comforting, because it's identifiable. That is, you can find comparable patterns when you look back.

An unpopular minority group's asserting its rights for equal treatment always prompts a backlash, every single time. It incites a death rattle of the desire not to change, to keep people in their place and marginalized, to prevent them from being equal.

Frankly, I interpret the strength of the popular reaction to same-sex marriage as a sign that we're making huge progress. It means that the issue is on the front burner, that people are paying attention and care. It means the debate that's going to shift this social institution is well under way.

The fact that marriage for same-sex couples hasn't yet achieved majority support isn't shocking, particularly when you measure what people do in the secrecy of the ballot box. Voting in private turns out not to be the same as what people say they'll do when their identity is known. Balloting is the last bastion of prejudice, in an ironic and sad way.

Interestingly, the Oregon Family Council's Tim Nashif supplied data supporting Kaiser's point.

A lot more people [in Oregon], at least three or four [percentage] points, voted yes on [Measure] 36 than were willing to say to pollsters that they would vote yes. The undecideds grew as we got into the campaign, which is very unusual. When there was no risk to say what your position was, the undecideds were only 4 or 5 percent on this issue. But when we got closer to the election, and the heat started getting turned up, the undecideds grew. That's a duplication of what took place in Louisiana, Michigan, Missouri, and Ohio.

Kaiser continued her analysis.

If you look around the country today, including our very "blue" state of California, when there are popular votes affecting the rights of racial minorities, quite often majorities will seek to disadvantage those groups, even though overt racial prejudice is now very socially unacceptable.

So I don't put a lot of stock in popular votes against same-sex marriage. They need to be understood in their historical context and as one segment of power wielding in a governmental system where power is exerted in multiple ways – through legislatures, courts, executives, and yes, even some popular votes.

San Francisco Supervisor Bevan Dufty also reflected on the validity of the backlash assertion.

There's been incredible movement on the part of the American people with regard to same-sex marriage, more than on most other issues I've seen. To have someone of such narrow mindset as our President start to talk positively about civil unions and domestic partnerships is unprecedented. To see someone who so clearly panders to uninformed religious zealotry and who then somehow makes those preelection utterances [on the *Good Morning America* broadcast of October 2004] is a sign of how powerful things are.

The Positive Effects of Goodridge

As chapter 3 reveals, the political impact of *Goodridge* at home in Massachusetts was titanic. The decisions radically changed the political and social landscape in the Commonwealth and fundamentally transformed the procedural dynamic in the legislature. While the Massachusetts gay and lesbian community would have been lucky to receive just domestic-partner health insurance benefits statewide before *Goodridge*, full civil unions with all the rights and responsibilities of marriage instantly became the political fallback position after the ruling.

Moreover, in just fifteen months, the composition of the two-hundred-seat General Court shifted to produce a net gain of eight votes favoring same-sex marriage, a remarkable statistic in light of the legislative incumbency effect. Yet the alteration in votes on the Travaglini-Lees Amendment was far more dramatic: from 105 in favor and 92 opposed in March 2004 to 157 opposed and just 37 in favor eighteen months later. Even though some of that change represented strategic switches by conservative legislators, the number of solid votes in favor of same-sex marriage increased by at least 23, and perhaps as much as 34, in the second ConCon.

What is more, a major new state interest group, MassEquality, whose sole purpose was to protect the *Goodridge* achievement, sprang up virtually overnight, raising more than two million dollars in less than a year in a state of 6.4 million residents.

Thus, a more comprehensive political transformation over a cutting-edge social issue in such a short time is hard to imagine.

Public opinion polling data from Massachusetts, however, offer a somewhat different picture. In April 2003, seven months prior to

Goodridge, the *Boston Globe* reported that 50 percent of Bay State residents supported, and 44 percent opposed, same-sex marriage (Phillips 2003). However, in February 2004, the same month as the second SJC ruling (*Opinions*), 53 percent of Massachusetts residents said they opposed gay marriage. Then, in March 2005, ten months after lesbian and gay weddings began there, 56 percent of residents were in favor (Greenberger 2005). This fluctuation in public attitudes isn't uncharacteristic of the general volatility of opinion, especially in times of significant legal and social transition. Recall that media attention to the San Francisco marriages flooded the nation in February 2004.

The positive impact of *Goodridge* outside Massachusetts was also substantial. Indeed, well-informed observers believe that none of the momentous events in 2004 surrounding same-sex marriage would have happened without *Goodridge*. Consider, for instance, Kate Kendell's assessment regarding San Francisco.

Kendell: Had it not been for Massachusetts, even considering the President's [2004] State of the Union in isolation, I don't think the mayor would have done what he did. Moreover, Bush might not have said what he did [in the address] without Massachusetts. After all, what else did his mentioning "activist judges" refer to?

I think that Mayor Newsom felt this was the way the issue was trending and that Massachusetts should not be out ahead of California. I think he felt that what he was doing was consistent with progressive ideology around equal protection of laws and full inclusion and fairness. The Massachusetts ruling provided a foundation for him to build on. It's my suspicion that he would not have done what he did if there were a complete vacuum.

Q: Consider the counterfactual that the Massachusetts court never decided the *Goodridge* case or one like it, for whatever reason. You don't think the mayor would have acted then in the same way?

A: I don't. To do it then would be much more rash. While I think he is brash and quite captivatingly naïve, in the sense of thinking that he can change the world, I just don't think it would have occurred to him in the same way to do this if Massachusetts weren't already out there.

Q: So Massachusetts was really a critical step for the mayor to do what he did?

A: I think that's right. It's a matter of pretty easily ascertainable supposition that, had we not had Massachusetts, Bush wouldn't have said what he said in the State of the Union. All of these things are related. If you take out Massachusetts, I think [2004] would have been much different, and much less interesting.

Aaron Peskin, president of San Francisco's Board of Supervisors, reinforced Kendell's judgment: "The Massachusetts state supreme court [*Goodridge*] decisions clearly gave Mayor Newsom license to commit an act of municipal civil disobedience in San Francisco." Indeed, the second decision in the *Goodridge* lineage (*Opinions*) was rendered just nine days before Newsom's public announcement.

Roey Thorpe of Basic Rights Oregon also noted the centrality of the Massachusetts rulings.

Because Oregon's Constitution is so much like Massachusetts', *Goodridge* was the icing on the cake. It was very important, especially in terms of our being able to convince the Multnomah County commissioners that they needed to look into the issue. One of the first things that they said to us was, "Well, we've investigated this question in the past." And we were able to respond, "You need to inquire again because of the *Goodridge* decision in Massachusetts."

Massachusetts was key, certainly in terms of the momentum that occurred nationally. I also think there was a shift in the consciousness of same-sex couples. The *Goodridge* decision just opened the floodgates of people's imaginations and of their sense of self-worth. I think that was transformational.

Indeed, same-sex couples who received marriage licenses during February and March of 2004 weighed in on the *Goodridge* impact. As the introductory chapter indicates, one of the sixty-four couples married in New Mexico explained how *Goodridge* clarified their perspective.

Greg: I had been putting a lot of thought into the whole marriage issue and talking to people. Some would say, "Civil unions, maybe. But I don't know. I just can't see same-sex marriage." Well, why? You know, the whole thing.

So then I just started thinking to myself about domestic partnerships, civil unions, and all of that, and the ways that can give me a lot of the things I may be looking for. But also wondering how it plays into this whole psychology.

But you know what? Anything less than marriage really isn't enough. If civil union has all the benefits – every single one – that marriage gives you, it's still a different word. It's a different psychological thing. As gay people, we are not the same. We're different. We're less. Even if they try to make them the same, it's still the perception of having less. So the psychology of that was already brewing. And then when the Massachusetts court decision was rendered and that language was used ["The history of our nation has demonstrated that separate is seldom, if ever, equal"], I was like, "Yes! That's *it!*"

Q: Do you think you would have reached the same realization without the Massachusetts case?

Greg: A lot of my thinking about the issue was generated by the possibility of its being real. And until the Massachusetts case, the reality of same-sex marriage seemed too far away for this country.

Craig: The legality thing was always ticking in the background, and I felt that the cards were really stacked against us. It wasn't until Massachusetts that I actually start thinking, "We may win this one."

Ranking Goodridge

One question asked of almost all interviewees sought to place *Goodridge* in comparative perspective: "If you were to think about all of the events around the country in the last year and a half with regard to same-sex marriage, and asked to rank order them in terms of importance, which would be number one? Which would be the most important?" A sampling of responses to that question from across the nation follows.

Sherri Sokeland Kaiser, the San Francisco deputy city attorney, first listed the finalists in the competition.

> The three contenders for the most important [same-sex marriage] event would be the marriages in San Francisco, the *Goodridge* pair of decisions, and the *Lawrence [v. Texas* (2003)] decision by

the U.S. Supreme Court. Historically speaking, the most importance may go to *Lawrence*, because I think it's going to usher in a
whole new era of jurisprudence on gay and lesbian rights.

But for now at least, it's *Goodridge*, because, on the issue of
same-sex marriage, nothing could be more important than having
a state that legally provides marriage to same-sex couples on the
basis of the very constitutional concerns that are being raised in
many other states. That precedent and the humanizing influence
it's going to have as more and more couples in Massachusetts get
married, and the sky doesn't fall, and marriage doesn't lose its
meaning for anyone .... . The more it just becomes an accepted
and normal and really unremarkable event in Massachusetts, the
more that's going to be an increasingly powerful example for
other states, such as California, to follow.

Diana in San Francisco:

Massachusetts. Definitely. It was a decision based upon careful
thought and deliberation about what we can do, given what our
Constitution says. There is more weight to that. People can dismiss all the things that Jason West and Gavin Newsom and others
did as rogue acts. Massachusetts wasn't outside the process. It was
within a process. A decision was made there in the way it should
be made. That was the most important.

Evan Wolfson, the person most credited as the principal architect
of gay people's struggle for legal access to the civil institution of
marriage in the United States, offered the following answer to the
question of most important event.

Getting people married, making it real. Real families, real couples,
really married. So you can look at May 17[, 2004,] and thereafter
in Massachusetts. You can look at Canada. You can look at some
of the other cities and jurisdictions. But I think that Massachusetts
probably is number one, because of the fact that it's unquestion-
able, undistracted, pure.

Mary Bonauto, the civil rights project director of GLAD and the
lead attorney for the *Goodridge* plaintiffs, summed up the case's
impact on elites.

186

Q: Let me direct your attention to another major research concern of mine, that is, *Goodridge* as a catalyst for the rest of the nation. My question is, but for *Goodridge*, would the things that happened in San Francisco and elsewhere around the country have occurred in the same way?

A: I do not personally know some important actors here, such as Gavin Newsom or Jason West, but I have been privy to plenty of confidential conversations about these matters. I think it is fair to say that this would not have happened but for *Goodridge*.

Yet there are other "but for" causes as well. With respect to Newsom and West, it's partly generational: Enough is enough. One of the wonderful things about *Goodridge* is that it was a new line in the sand. The court said, we've looked at every argument, and they all fail as a matter of logic. *Goodridge* said that we're taking a sharp turn in a different direction. And I think there are other people who have just been longing for that day.

I've talked for many years about the [California Supreme Court's] *Perez* [v. *Sharp* (1948)] decision [the first by a court of last resort to strike down a state prohibition on interracial marriage], in the sense that I assumed that there was some group of people who thought this kind of discrimination was outrageous, and finally, a court said so, even though all the polls stunk and all the previous court decisions were awful. *Plessy* [v. *Ferguson* (1896)] was still the law of the land, and even post-*Perez*, there were all these appeals until *Loving* [v. *Virginia* (1967)]. So I always hoped that we'd get to that point, too, where some court finally said, come on, this is about equality, this is about dignity. So gay people, too. And that would be a catalyst.

I think that's what happened. I see *Goodridge* as a beacon of hope, of fairness and equality, going out to the world for people who are ready to hear it. In that sense, I think it touched Newsom and others.

Interviewing fifty married same-sex couples around the country, I found among them empirical indicators of *Goodridge*'s impact at the grass roots. Numerous couples without prior interest in law, for example, revealed that they had read the decision. Some Massachusetts pairs watched all of the proceedings of the televised state constitutional convention in February and March 2004, and most knew the names and issue positions of their state representatives.

Expectations also increased from the bottom up. Before November 2003, most couples would have accepted civil unions without question. Today, however, they are almost universally rejected, condemned as markers of second-class citizenship. A Massachusetts gay man put it memorably.

Q: What came out of the [2004] Constitutional Convention was a hybrid. Marriage would be defined as only between one man and one woman, but at the same time, the amendment would create civil unions for gays with all the same rights of marriage, basically.
A: It's the "basically" part that concerns me. [Mockingly, like a car-selling politician:] "*Basically*, it's going to be the same thing, awright. This Yugo is basically *just like* a Cadillac. That is, if you put gas in it, it *goes.*" That's my response to civil unions.

A working-class lesbian couple from a Boston suburb reinforced the expectational change.

Marianne: All of a sudden [at the end of 2003], people here started to realize, "Wow! We *could* get married." Before that, we would've actually been satisfied with civil unions.
Christine: We *would* have been satisfied with civil unions. We would 'a' been clickin' our heels, thinking we'd arrived. We thought that Vermont was nirvana.
Marianne: Absolutely!
Christine: We fantasized about retiring in Vermont, where we'd have us a civil union.
Marianne: Can you imagine if they had "given" us civil unions?
Christine: Now it's like, civil unions? [and flicks her hand in dismissal].
Marianne: How do you like them apples! Who wants civil unions when you can have marriage?
Q: So what happened here in Massachusetts really raised your consciousness?
Marianne: Positively.
Christine: Absolutely. And our sense of entitlement

Table 7.1 summarizes the responses of the couples to the question about the most important same-sex marriage event.

Table 7.1. *Answers to the question "What was the most important same-sex marriage event?"*

	Events in Massachusetts	Events in San Francisco	Events in Oregon	Events in New Paltz
All 74 respondents	59 (80%)	11 (15%)	3 (4%)	1 (1%)
25 Massachusetts respondents	24 (96%)	1 (4%)		
28 Oregon respondents	20 (71%)	5 (18%)	3 (11%)	
19 San Francisco respondents	13 (68%)	5 (26%)		1 (5%)
All 49 non-Massachusetts respondents	35 (71%)	10 (20%)	3 (6%)	1 (2%)
All 39 gay male respondents	32 (82%)	5 (13%)	1 (3%)	1 (3%)
All 35 lesbian respondents	27 (77%)	6 (17%)	2 (6%)	

Of course, the pairs who married in Massachusetts, San Francisco, Portland, and elsewhere may not accurately reflect the opinion of all lesbian and gay Americans. Indeed, the LGBT community does not even monolithically support access to civil marriage. A San Francisco group called Gay Shame, for instance, actively opposes the idea of gays marrying. Nonetheless, national LGBT interest groups, collectively with annual incomes in excess of $50 million (Cahill 2004: 21), endorse marriage rights for same-sex couples. Thus, one can reasonably infer that the overwhelming majority of lesbian and gay Americans do aspire to legal equality in terms of the right to marry. My snapshot of their opinion regarding a *Goodridge* effect is a reasonable estimation of the population, taking into account the challenges of its identification referred to in the Appendix.

Almost 80 percent of the married lesbians and gay men surveyed around the country think that the same-sex marriage events in Massachusetts during 2003 and 2004 were the most important for achieving their social goal. Yet this proportion may be skewed, because 25 (34%) of the respondents were themselves from Massachusetts and may therefore reflect parochial bias. Indeed,

96 percent of Massachusetts residents pointed to their own state's actions as the most important nationwide, just as some Oregonians were the only respondents to think the Multnomah County events were the most consequential. This potential parochialism can be corrected by looking at only the 49 respondents from outside the Bay State, all of whom live in the West. Remarkably, 71 percent of Westerners still ranked Massachusetts first, despite the substantial media attention to the marriages in San Francisco, Portland, and elsewhere. Even more strikingly, 68 percent of married lesbian and gay San Franciscans thought *Goodridge* was more significant than what their own beloved mayor did.

A second question asked of married same-sex couples that is relevant to the *Goodridge* effect was: "Have the events involving same-sex marriage around the country in the last year or so made you more politically involved?" Table 7.2 summarizes the responses.

Couples manifested their greater political involvement in several ways. The most common indicator was making financial donations to interest groups, either for the first time or increasing past contribution amounts. The second most frequent activity was contacting elected representatives. A more limited group participated in public demonstrations for the first time. In the two states (Massachusetts and Oregon) with active political campaigns in 2004 concerning same-sex marriage, a small number of respondents volunteered time in those efforts. One lesbian couple in Oregon told a story of campaigning door-to-door in the Portland suburbs.

Table 7.2. *Answers to the question "As a result of same-sex marriage events, have you been more politically involved?"*

	No	Yes
All 72 respondents	41 (57%)	31 (43%)
18 Massachusetts respondents	6 (33%)	12 (67%)
32 Oregon respondents	20 (63%)	12 (38%)
22 San Francisco respondents	15 (68%)	7 (32%)
All 54 non-Massachusetts respondents	35 (65%)	19 (35%)
All 39 gay male respondents	21 (54%)	18 (46%)
All 33 lesbian respondents	20 (61%)	13 (39%)

Doubtless, the sample sizes of respondents here are small. Moreover, as outlined in the Appendix, the sampling techniques varied somewhat across states. In particular, the San Francisco respondents may not be as representative of the larger population as the other groups are. In addition, the question asked of respondents was comparative in degree and not absolute. So some answered that they were already so politically involved that it was difficult, if not impossible, for them to do more.

Nonetheless, these data suggest that the surge of official activity on same-sex marriage in 2003–2004 inspired lesbians and gay men who married in Massachusetts to greater political action (67%) than their counterparts in either Oregon (38%) or San Francisco (32%).

Regardless of state-specific differences, however, key observers confirmed the general finding of increased political activism. David Owen, San Francisco Supervisor Aaron Peskin's chief legislative aid, elaborated.

> I grew up in an upper-middle-class family and had a lot of breaks, but I was in the closet for a long time. Aside from the obvious elements of enduring disinformation and nonacceptance, I never experienced a time when I felt as though the government was actually targeting me, trying to take away rights that could be mine – until now.
>
> I think lots of gay people who found themselves in similar situations had the same feeling when this happened, when on election day in thirteen states [in 2004], American citizens actually voted to officially take away rights that could be ours. That resonated with lesbians and gay men. They learned something fundamental from that.

San Francisco Supervisor Bevan Dufty:

> I think there's a positive reason for gay people to be politically involved now. There's always been a core of activism in the community. But marriage touched a deeper essence that made us hopeful and want to do things.
>
> And I think it was a huge benefit for [2004 Democratic Presidential Nominee John] Kerry. Let me tell you, I exported people

from my [legislative] district all over the country. I did a press conference at the Harvey Milk MUNI [San Francisco municipal railway, or subway] station ten days before the [November general] election. The number of gay people I saw rolling their bags and saying, "I'm going to Ohio" [to get out the vote] or "I'm going to Nevada" [to electioneer], was astounding. Democrats should be thanking us for how same-sex marriage motivated this vital core of party workers and voters.

So I think marriage equality has given lesbians and gay men a positive reason to be involved, something that fighting either the AIDS epidemic or employment discrimination didn't do in the same way. It's really helped raise consciousness, so that gay people see clearly where they stand in the American political universe.

Conclusion

Goodridge brought about enormous social change. An estimated 6,000 or more lesbian and gay couples married in Massachusetts in the year following May 17, 2004. Moreover, although state supreme courts invalidated the 7,000-plus ceremonies performed in San Francisco and Portland, the Massachusetts marriages are unassailable as a legal matter. Even Bay State gay-marriage opponents who seek a constitutional amendment banning such nuptials (and not authorizing civil unions), by means of a citizen initiative on the 2008 state ballot, concede that the measure would not be retroactive. Thus, a sizable population of legally married same-sex couples exists in the United States for the first time, all thanks alone to the SJC's action.

Equally important, *Goodridge* had a profound inspirational effect for the marriage movement, among elites and the grass roots, at home and beyond. The rulings instituted fundamental change in Massachusetts politics. Virtually overnight, *Goodridge* upended the procedural posture of the marriage debate in the Bay State and empowered those who had been politically weak before the decisions. Then, through the consequential efforts of MassEquality, the state legislature became substantially more progressive as a result of the 2004–2005 elections. Indeed, the Boston media intimated that the way the controversy over same-sex marriage played out in the Bay State helped to topple its conservative house Speaker.

In addition, the same-sex weddings in San Francisco, Portland, and elsewhere would not have occurred without the example of *Goodridge*. As Kate Kendell and Roey Thorpe suggest, Mayor Newsom and the Multnomah County commissioners would not have acted as boldly as they did in a national legal vacuum regarding same-sex marriage.

Finally, *Goodridge* radicalized and coalesced the gay community like no other event since the advent of AIDS in the 1980s. Time and again, same-sex couples volunteered in interviews across the nation that they never expected marriage to be available to them during their lifetimes. Yet *Goodridge* opened a floodgate of heightened expectations. Where once civil unions sparked fantasies of retirement in Vermont, now those erstwhile special opportunities were dismissed as symbols of second-class citizenship. What is more, as the data in Table 7.2 intimate, *Goodridge* prompted some lesbians and gay men to political action. At least a third of respondents reported increased activism, with the magnitude perhaps as high as two-thirds in Massachusetts itself.

These findings diminish the perception that courts are hollow hopes for significant social reform. With nearly all other state and national policy makers at odds with its goal, the Massachusetts Supreme Judicial Court nonetheless achieved singular success in expanding the ambit of who receives the benefits of getting married in America, in inspiring political elites elsewhere in the country to follow suit, and in mobilizing grass-roots supporters to entrench their legal victory politically.

Methods

TO GATHER MATERIAL FOR THE BOOK, I conducted eighty-five in-depth interviews in California, Massachusetts, New Mexico, New York, and Oregon. I met with public officials (county clerks, mayors, city council members, city attorneys, and state legislators) who participated directly in the sundry same-sex marriage events of 2004. I also interviewed interest group representatives on both sides of the marriage controversy, as well as lesbian and gay couples who wed or sought to. This volume reports on both qualitative and quantitative results from that research.

Identifying the relevant political elites was fairly straightforward. Massachusetts state legislators, for example, were the nonjudicial officials most conspicuously involved with the issue of same-sex marriage in that commonwealth. The mayors of San Francisco and New Paltz, New York, were the key actors there, as was the clerk in Sandoval County, New Mexico. Statewide lesbian and gay organizations often spearheaded or bolstered these officials' efforts to issue marriage licenses to same-sex couples, while state "family councils" or "family institutes" frequently opposed such endeavors.

Yet sampling lesbian and gay Americans at the grass roots is inherently challenging:

> The most difficult part of research directly investigating gays and lesbians is identifying lesbians and gays. The gay and lesbian population is "invisible." Whether a researcher meets someone face to face, makes phone contact, or gives out anonymous confidential questionnaires, that researcher remains at the mercy of the participant to self-identify as lesbian or gay. (Riggle and Tadlock 1999: 6)

Nonetheless, I was able to surmount this problem because my research focused on a discrete subpopulation: lesbian and gay couples who married. Several sources helped to identify this group. The clerks in both Multnomah County, Oregon, and San Francisco, for example, sell lists of the names and addresses of the same-sex couples who married there. In Massachusetts, I chose a sample of cities and towns representing a variety of socioeconomic categories (working class, more middle class, etc.) and then visited the clerks of those communities to request the names and addresses of all same-sex couples who applied for marriage licenses there on May 7, 2004, the first day they were offered to gay and lesbian pairs. Finally, I searched the Internet for media coverage of couples in New Mexico who married in Sandoval County.

I also made efforts to secure random samples of the couples, although the challenges to do so were substantial. For the Multnomah County list of just over 3,000, for instance, I sent written invitations to interview to approximately eighty in the metropolitan Portland area. In order to sample people throughout the entire seven-week period of marriages there, I selected the first couples listed for each of those thirty-five business days. Then, since the overwhelming number of applications occurred in the first few days and weeks that licenses were offered, I chose every tenth couple during that time to determine the remaining forty-five invited to interview. I deviated slightly from these procedures in order to achieve a balance between male and female couples.

I followed a similar process for San Francisco's list of 4,037 couples, except that I was able to interview only within a relatively small area of the city. Without outside funding for my research, I personally bore all the expense of travel and lodging to conduct interviews. As a result, I could not afford to rent a car to drive throughout the Bay Area (as I did in Portland). So I limited the geographic boundaries to what I could walk to from the home of the friend with whom I stayed or what otherwise was reasonably reachable by public transportation.

Fortunately in Massachusetts, I was able to housesit for a vacationing Wellesley College faculty member for over a month and had my own car to drive. So I was able to maneuver without limitation throughout the eastern half of the Commonwealth.

Accordingly, I think that my sample is reasonably representative of the population of lesbian and gay couples who married.

Of course, the nature of the interview process is that all subjects are ultimately self-selected. For instance, I sent invitations to interview to thirty Massachusetts state legislators, but just seven agreed to meet with me. Likewise, between 20 and 25 percent of the gay and lesbian pairs responded favorably to my interview requests.

References

Adams v. Howerton. 1980. 486 F.Supp. 1119.

Akers, Joshua. 2004. "GOP Says Sandoval Clerk 'A Disgrace.'" *Albuquerque Journal*, April 21.

Andersen, Ellen Ann. 2005. *Out of the Closets and into the Courts.* Ann Arbor: University of Michigan Press.

Badgett, M. V. Lee, and R. Bradley Sears. 2005. "Putting a Price on Equality? The Impact of Same-Sex Marriage on California's Budget." *Stanford Law & Policy Review* 16: 197.

Baehr v. Lewin. 1993. 74 Haw. 645, 852 P.2d 44.

Baker v. Nelson. 1971. 191 N.W.2d 185.

Baker v. State. 1999. 170 Vt. 194, 744 A.2d 864.

Belluck, Pam. 2004. "Maybe Same-Sex Marriage Didn't Make the Difference." *New York Times*, November 7, p. WK5.

Bowers v. Hardwick. 1986. 478 U.S. 186.

Cahill, Sean. 2004. *Same-Sex Marriage in the United States: Focus on the Facts.* Lanham, Md.: Lexington Books.

Campbell, David E., and J. Quin Monson. 2005. "The Religion Card: Evangelicals, Catholics, and Gay Marriage in the 2004 Presidential Election." Presented at the annual meeting of the American Political Science Association, Washington, D.C.

Canon, Bradley C. 1998. "The Supreme Court and Policy Reform: *The Hollow Hope* Revisited." In Schultz, *Leveraging the Law.*

Coordination Proceeding. 2005. 2005 WL 583129.

Dahl, Robert A. 1957. "Decision-Making in a Democracy: The Supreme Court as a National Policy-Maker." *Journal of Public Law* 6: 279.

De Santo v. Barnsley. 1984. 476 A.2d 952.

Dean v. District of Columbia. 1992. 18 FLR 1141.

Duberman, Martin. 1993. *Stonewall.* New York: Dutton.

Dupuis, Martin. 2002. *Same-Sex Marriage, Legal Mobilization, and the Politics of Rights.* New York: Peter Lang.

Ebbert, Stephanie. 2002. "Horse Lovers Say They Were Duped." *Boston Globe*, March 26, p. B2.

Eskridge, William N., Jr. 1999. *Gaylaw: Challenging the Apartheid of the Closet.* Cambridge, Mass.: Harvard University Press.

Garrow, David J. 2004. "Toward a More Perfect Union." *New York Times Magazine*, May 9, p. 52.

Gerstmann, Evan. 2005. "Litigating Same-Sex Marriage: Might the Courts Actually Be Bastions of Rationality?" *PS: Political Science and Politics* 38: 217.

Goodridge v. Department of Public Health. 2003. 440 Mass. 309, 798 N.E.2d 941.

Greenberger, Scott S. 2005. "One Year Later, Nation Divided on Gay Marriage." *Boston Globe*, May 15.

"Group Drops Bid to Ban Same-Sex Marriage." 2005. *New York Times*, December 29, p. A24.

Hillygus, D. Sunshine, and Todd G. Shields. 2005. "Moral Issues and Voter Decision Making in the 2004 Presidential Election." *PS: Political Science and Politics* 38: 201.

Jones v. Hallahan. 1973. 501 S.W.2d 588.

Klein, Ethel D. 2005. "The Anti-Gay Backslash?" In H. N. Hirsch ed., *The Future of Gay Rights in America*. New York: Routledge.

Kuykendall, Mae. 2001. "Gay Marriages and Civil Unions: Democracy, the Judiciary, and Discursive Space in the Liberal Society." *Mercer Law Review* 52: 1003.

Lawrence v. Texas. 2003. 539 U.S. 558.

LeBlanc, Steve. 2005. "Massachusetts Legislature Rejects Proposed Amendment Banning Gay Marriage." *Boston Globe*, September 14.

Lewis, Gregory B. 2005. "Same-Sex Marriage and the 2004 Presidential Election." *PS: Political Science and Politics* 38: 195.

Lewis, Raphael. 2004. "A Rift on Gay Unions Fuels a Coup at Polls." *Boston Globe*, September 26.

Li v. State. 2005. 338 Or. 376, 110 P.3d 91.

Lockyer v. City and County of San Francisco. 2004. 33 Cal.4th 1055, 95 P.3d 459.

Loving v. Virginia. 1967. 388 U.S. 1.

Marotta, Toby. 1981. *The Politics of Homosexuality*. Boston: Houghton Mifflin.

McCann, Michael W. 1994. *Rights at Work: Pay Equity Reform and the Politics of Legal Mobilization*. Chicago: University of Chicago Press.

McGivern, Tim. 2004. "Defining Marriage." *Weekly Alibi*, March 11–17.

Medina, Jennifer. 2005. "Charges Dropped against Mayor Who Performed Gay Weddings." *New York Times*, July 13, p. B5.

Merrick v. Board of Higher Education. 1992. 116 Or.App. 258, 841 P.2d 646.

Moats, David. 2004. *Civil Wars: A Battle for Gay Marriage*. Orlando, Fla.: Harcourt.

Murphy, Dean E. 2005. "Schwarzenegger to Veto Same-Sex Marriage Bill." *New York Times*, September 8, p. A18.

Opinions of the Justices to the Senate. 2004. 440 Mass. 1201, 802 N.E.2d 565.

Ottenheimer, Martin. 1996. *Forbidden Relatives: The American Myth of Cousin Marriage*. Champaign: University of Illinois Press.

Perez v. Sharp. 1948. 32 Cal.2d 711, 198 P.2d 17.

Phillips, Frank. 2003. "Support for Gay Marriage: Mass. Poll Finds Half in Favor." *Boston Globe*, April 8.

Phillips, Frank. 2004. "Prospects Shift as DiMasi Takes over for Finneran." *Boston Globe*, September 28.

Pinello, Daniel R. 2003. *Gay Rights and American Law*. New York: Cambridge University Press.

Plessy v. Ferguson. 1896. 163 U.S. 537.

Reed, Douglas S. 1999. "Popular Constitutionalism: Toward a Theory of State Constitutional Meanings." *Rutgers Law Journal* 30: 871.

Riggle, Ellen D. B., and Barry L. Tadlock. 1999. "Gays and Lesbians in the Democratic Process: Past, Present, and Future." In Ellen D. B. Riggle and Barry L. Tadlock (eds.), *Gays and Lesbians in the Democratic Process: Public Policy, Public Opinion, and Political Representation*. New York: Columbia University Press.

Rosenberg, Gerald N. 1991. *The Hollow Hope: Can Courts Bring about Social Change?* Chicago: University of Chicago Press.

Scheingold, Stuart A. 1974. *The Politics of Rights: Lawyers, Public Policy and Political Change*. New Haven, Conn.: Yale University Press.

Schultz, David A., ed. 1998. *Leveraging the Law: Using the Courts to Achieve Social Change*. New York: Peter Lang.

Sherrill, Kenneth. 2005. "Same-sex Marriage, Civil Unions, and the 2004 Presidential Vote." In H. N. Hirsch, ed., *The Future of Gay Rights in America*. New York: Routledge.

Shorto, Russell. 2005. "What's Their Real Problem with Gay Marriage? (It's the Gay Part)." *New York Times Magazine*, June 19, p. 34.

Singer v. Hara. 1974. 11 Wash.App. 247, 522 P.2d 1187.

Staszewski, Glen. 2005. "The Bait-and-Switch in Direct Democracy." Manuscript, Michigan State University College of Law.

Sullivan, Andrew, ed. 2004. *Same-Sex Marriage: Pro and Con. A Reader*. New York: Vintage.

Wolfson, Evan. 2004. *Why Marriage Matters: America, Equality, and Gay People's Right to Marry*. New York: Simon & Schuster.

Index